ARCHITECTURE
OF
CREATIVITY:

Profiles Behind The Mask

ARCHITECTURE OF CREATIVITY:

Profiles Behind The Mask

Ronald Turco, MD

Dancing Moon Press
Yachats, Oregon

Library of Congress Catalog Card Number: 98-73836
Turco, Ronald
Architecture of Creativity / Turco, Ronald
ISBN 1-892076-03-93
Title.

Manufactured in the United States of America

FIRST EDITION

For

ANNYCE AND DIANA

*"If I could write the beauty of your eyes
And in fresh numbers number all your graces,
The age to come would say, "This poet lies—
Such heavenly touches ne'er touched earthly faces."*

– Shakespeare

OTHER BOOKS BY THE AUTHOR

The Kennedy Memorandum: A Technical Analysis of the Kennedy Assassination, 1985 – Gleneden Press

Fibromyalgia: Somatization—The Humpty Dumpty Syndrome, 1990 – Gleneden Press

Closely Watched Shadows, 1998 – BookPartners
1998 – Dancing Moon Press

CONTENTS

INTRODUCTION

This book is written for reader enjoyment and is designed so that each chapter may be read independently. There is no special reason for the selection of the subjects. It would be impossible to include all the artists that readers or the author have an interest in and those selected are representative of a wide range of creativity. The final common denominator is that we are all human. Artists share our aspirations, frailties, joys and sorrows. These profiles of the artists are not meant to be a complete analysis of their personalities. No single theoretical model, such as psychoanalysis, can accomplish such a task without a "face-to-face" relationship with the individual. A lengthy psychoanalysis in person is necessary before arriving at a reasonable understanding of anyone. Readers should form their own opinions about the validity or applicability of my interpretations; they will certainly discover my perspective. A contemporary television news network has as its slogan, "We report, you decide" and I have tried to follow this credo.

A list of sources associated with each chapter is provided at the end of this volume. Research for this book is not limited to items on this source reading material list. My research encompasses thirty years of museum study, lectures and seminars on psychoanalysis and creativity, numerous interviews with artists and scholars and evening attendance at art classes conducted by The Pacific Northwest College of Art.

The Architecture of Creativity is an ideal book for group discussion in either small informal groups or in structured seminars. I've included many points of controversy and divergences of opinion that should stimulate even the most composed recreational reader, student or critic. Most of this work is designed to promote emotional as well as intellectual stimulation and controversy. If that occurs I will have achieved my purpose.

I wish to thank Carla Perry for her diligence and organizing skills, Joanne for her encouragement and penetrating intellect, and Louie for his patience and devotion.

Ronald Turco
Portland, Oregon 1998

HAIKU

Rain and trees
Mostly feeling
of Creation

Summer mist
Warm rain
Bright sun

Brown and green
Tall pines
Walking bear

Kinkaju-Ji temple
Clouds, mist, children
I am them

-Ronald Turco, 1998

1

ABSTRACTIONS
AND
INNER REALITY

To see a world in a grain of sand,
And a heaven in a wild flower,
Hold infinity in the palm of your hand,
And eternity in an hour.

– William Blake
"Auguries of Innocence"

Our imagination allows us to grasp the reality of existence. Imagination is the product of our consciousness and our unconscious thought processes. We live in an inner reality where the past is always present and the future possibly so. Modern physics has taught that we cannot separate the "reality" of what is "outside" from our inner life, and nowhere is this more true than in the subjective experience of art. We are part of the interplay of experience, mind and reality. What we "see" is what we "are." The abstractions of our thoughts are apart from concrete existence yet include the mental involvement of thought and imagination in the object, the work of art. This experience reaches its highest artistic expression in abstract art free of representational content. It is the abstraction of thought that separates the inherent qualities or properties from the actual physical concept. Simply stated, we bring ourselves to the artistic work. We become part of the art work if we suspend thought and bring ourselves to the work with a "beginner's mind." We can then see the creation for what it is.

Artistic creativity is a result of the complex interplay of intellectual, cognitive and affective processes with the intuitive ability to discern truth. Truth is beauty. The experience of beauty, perhaps originally sensual, becomes an abstraction. The artist with his brush strokes, the musician with his notes, the writer with his words, indeed, even the statesman with his ideas, makes a statement and announces his/her intent to the universe. This process unfolds as sure as day follows night. The artists' inner self resonates with external reality.

We appreciate the products of artistic labor because, largely through unconscious mental processes, we sense our own inner reality and experience. In essence "A kiss is still a kiss." The work strikes a cord within.

In the penultimate experience, art is not just a pretty picture, stories not just entertainment, music not just distraction. Unknowingly, we fuse with the product—we become one with the total experience. The work "talks" to us. We don't *have* to think about it, although we may. We don't *have* to like it, although we most likely will. We *experience art*. If we are free—that is, if we allow ourselves an opportunity to live in the moment, we become liberated. Our inner world experience is then one of abstractions and illusions. We live and experience through the uniqueness of our character and the uniqueness life has to offer. Sensing a glimpse of our true selves, we are primed for peak experience and wonderment. Defenses are down and antennae up.

Sigmund Freud described how jokes present us with the truth by catching us off guard and making us laugh. The artist does the same thing with his representations. He circumvents our barriers and talks to our unconscious. We understand, we appreciate—whether we want to or not. We are part of the artistic producer—part of the unfolding process of creativity. Part of the reality of creation. What we, as observers, bring to the work is what matters. Art is for *us*—for all creation. We can respect all creation.

Art then, is an expression of our uniqueness—our individuality and our shared humanity. It addresses what we share—our aspirations and fears, our hopes and dreams and our sense of purpose and standing in the universe. It teaches us how we are alike and how we are different. We all must die—but we must also live and share. While we live, art tells us where we have been, where we are and, sometimes, where we must go. It nurtures, soothes and informs. It defines our existence as humans. We listen with our "third" ear and, thus, we are able to rise above the mundaneness of everyday life.

Artistic experience and sensitivity are traced back to the child's first relationship and earliest experiences. D.W. Winnicott, a psychoanalyst, called attention to the *transitional object* of a child. The transitional object is a part of the early developmental experience of the self and is part self and part non-self. It evokes the relationship with the mother. This is the teddy bear or blanket we are familiar with and belongs to us as children yet is part of the outside world. The transitional object is thought by psychoanalysts to be the precursor of the adult's investment in cultural objects. This is a very important concept and the attachment to the transitional object is a normal, healthy and common experience. A Jungian psychologist might call this the "archetype" of an aesthetic object.

Once again we meet up with imagination and its investment in this object and the later development of artistic fantasy. Fantasy and reality thus become related. Freud saw in art the opportunity to fulfill wishes and to allow the expression of internal experiences. The artist may turn away from reality but find his way back through fantasy.

He uses his special gifts to give something valued as part of reality. (On a deeper level we speak of the replacement of the pleasure principle by the reality principle). Products of the imagination thus represent wishes being fulfilled both for the artist and the recipient. This is partly because symbols and substitutes can evoke emotion. Art combines a wish-fulfilling desire and reality. And, this is the real significance of art.

Ellen Handler Spitz wrote in her book, *Art And Psyche*, "A fundamental concept in psychoanalytic theory is that the human psyche never "gives up" anything. What is lost is, in fact, not lost but retained in another form, substituted for by something else…. The most persistent themes and imagery with which the artist is preoccupied ultimately derive, though in endlessly changing forms, from *the first five or six years of life*" (italics added).

Psychoanalyst Phyllis Greenacre noted that creative persons often develop a *family romance* in which they fantasize a different set of parents—perhaps more noble and exalted ones—and develop a sense of being special or chosen. These fantasies deeply imprint the lives of gifted people. A more important contribution Greenacre made involves her observation that artistically gifted children have a more intense sensitivity to sensory stimulation and react more intensely to smells, sounds touch and taste. She called this range of experience the *collective alternates*. Experiences originate in the relationship with the mother but become detached later and may be substituted. This is the *love affair with the world* that gifted children and artists experience. This theory is so important that Greenacre considers it indispensable in the development of artistic talent. The collective alternates offer the artist a sense of freedom. I refer to them as "creative alternatives" since the artist has many alternatives available to express himself.

Gifted children leave open avenues of problem solving. They deal with alternatives, and thus the modes of expression are more varied and creative. The work of art becomes a gift and in Greenacre's words a "love gift." The artist, open to a wide range of experiences, produces something special. The material the artist uses comes from deep within—from childhood and from primitive parts of the psyche. These are experiences many of us repress but the artist works with them and pursues a search for truth and expression. What is self-experience for the artist becomes experience for us all. The artist attempts to master inner conflicts and experiences what many of us simply ignore. The artist discovers and expresses his experiences and we all benefit. Although the artist may not be aware of the internal issues with which he is struggling, he is responding to psychological experiences from deep within his unconscious. The unconscious represents the creative drive, and thus artists see the world differently from most people and the creative outlet is a constructive path for the expression of the artists' unconscious. The objects created are sophisticated versions of the original transitional object of the child and give pleasure by allowing the inner world—unacceptable to many— to be available through illusion without conflict. The audience is invited to view and study the work by shaping internal images that are, ultimately, universal.

2

THE CREATION
OF MOOD:
ANDREW WYETH

"I have a strong romantic fantasy about things, and that's what I paint, but I come to it through realism. If you don't back up your dreams with truth, you have a very round-shouldered art... If somehow I can, before I leave this earth, combine my absolutely mad freedom and excitement with truth, then I will have done something."

– Andrew Wyeth

The well known New Orleans artist William "Billy" Solitario once described Andrew Wyeth to me as "a superb draftsman." Somewhat startled, I withdrew and a few days later called him on it. He explained that his statement was the supreme compliment for a man who could depict not only the realism and honesty—the truth—of life, but could also capture the essence of the spirit—the life of his subjects. It is this creation of mood and space that helps make Wyeth a wonder. As a former Pennsylvania boy, my perceptions of Wyeth's work go far beyond the pictorial representations. His work has all the meaning of a Rothko or Matisse, yet his is a meaning we can be part of without the need to "understand." Wyeth's work is intuitive.

Robert Hughes, an art critic, described Wyeth's work as "The tasteful, closeted, Puritan-wistful way..." and this is an oversimplification. He describes "...the images of hardscrabble Puritan rectitude, tinged with close-lipped sentimentality." Another art critic, William Fleming regards Wyeth's work as "...evocations of social decay and unfulfilled aspirations of life in the American scene." Both critics have mis-interpreted and under-interpreted Wyeth's work.

Andrew Wyeth is perhaps the most celebrated realist painter in the United States. The Maine and Pennsylvania scenes may appear detached, but on closer examination they reveal an intense emotional involvement with the subjects and their representations. His dry-brush watercolors are masterpieces and have inspired a generation of painters since his first public acclaim in 1937.

Although much of Wyeth's paintings has focused on the Kuerner farm in Chadds Ford, Pennsylvania and the farm belonging to Christina Olson and her brother Alvaro in Cushing, Maine, the work is universally manifested by symbolic content—"both private and universal"—that has a transcendent quality never fully apparent. The artist is obviously strongly connected (emotionally) to his subjects. The art depicts the reality of existence in all its multiple manifestations and the inevitable change we all experience.

Wyeth spent thirty years painting the Olsons and their farm, with his best known work represented by *Christina's World* (1948). The objects belonging to the Olsons'—rope, farm equipment, outbuildings—became "...metaphorical portraits of the Olsons." He continued to paint the objects until the summer of 1967, but when the Olsons died, Wyeth said he then found the objects "...not emotionally interesting." Hughes remarks of *Christina's World* that "...his subtly ominous painting of a polio-crippled girl gazing at a distant house and apparently crawling toward it vies with American Gothic in popularity." He interprets Wyeth's work as representing "...austerely dun and gray realist pictures of reclusive New Englanders, bleached frame houses, and open windows with lace curtains blowing a little spookily in the wind." More accurate is art historian and author John Canaday's description of Wyeth's realism, "...meticulous rendering of quiet subjects is deceptive, concealing as it does—or revealing as it does, for those who know how to see a picture—*the most acute perceptions of personality*, of the life in inanimate objects as ordinary as a weathered door." He has captured the essence of the artist's genius. Wyeth also used space and object dislocation as a means of producing an interior mood—classic modalities of painting for realism and anticlassic productions. He uses theme, technique and space to produce an atmosphere of timelessness and intensity.

The odd angles of some of his paintings also are provocative of transcendentalistic experience—what is real and what is beyond real—the ideal...the Platonic experience. Wyeth's watercolors have been described as progressing out of the primitive with their fluidity and luminosity. There is a dreamlike surrealism associated with this luminosity and transparency. His work remains controversial and some critics attempt to denigrate it and the artist by referring to opportunism, preferring the less intelligible, obtuse works of American abstract expressionists. Perhaps *Christina's World* is too much of a universal symbol for some—too real for the critics because of its representation of *the human condition.* This represents the "tragedy and joy" of life. Wyeth himself spoke of the poetic and "close scrutiny."

The intensity of detail in Wyeth's paintings convey the sense of vastness, isolation and loneliness. The work is quintessentially American. Wyeth described this well: "Maine, to me, is almost like going to the surface of the moon. I feel things are just hanging on the surface and that it's all going to blow away. In Maine, everything seems to be dwindling with terrific speed. In Pennsylvania, there's a substantial foundation underneath; depths of dirt and earth. Up in Maine, I feel it's all dry bones and desiccated sinews. That's actually the difference between the two places to me." Thomas Hoving writes of how he overcame his "sophistication," took off the blinders and became captured by the *"spiritual realism"* of *Christina's World.* Wyeth wrote, "Art, too, is seeing. I think you have got to use your eyes as well as your emotion, and one without the other just doesn't work. That's my art."

I met Andrew Wyeth on two occasions and I'm sure he would not remember either one. The first occurred in 1966 or 1967 during my medical-surgical training at the Bryn Mawr Hospital outside Philadelphia. Wyeth often visited his sick friend Christian Sanderson and we on the staff were very impressed with his devotion and the quiet sense of presence he brought to the hospital. The second occasion occurred at the Brandywine Museum. I had purchased a portrait of Wyeth by his son Jamie and found myself standing behind Andrew Wyeth himself. Once again his sense of "presence" was awesome.

Andrew Wyeth was born in Chadds Ford, Pennsylvania in 1917. His art training was received from his father N.C. Wyeth, a painter and illustrator. Andrew considered himself self-taught and during his formative years frequently visited Maine to be with his father. They loved Maine. He was also strongly influenced by the work of Winslow Homer. By 1937, Wyeth's reputation as a watercolorist was established with his first one-man show in New York.

In 1939 he began to use *tempera*—which has associations with the earth. "I think the real reason tempera fascinated me was that I loved the quality of the colors: the earth colors, the terra verde, the ochers, the reds...I really like tempera because it has a cocoon-like feeling of gray lostness—almost a lonely feeling." The evocation of earth. "A lot of people say I've brought realism back.... I honestly consider myself an abstractionist." Nevertheless Wyeth draws his themes from his surroundings and paints them with an intensity of drama unsurpassed by contemporary or classical artists. "The thing that makes me hang on to tempera is that if a picture does come off, it has a power and a solidity nothing else has...." I think one's art goes as far and as deep as one's love goes."

The tempera paintings are the milestones in his development. These dry mineral pigments are ground to a fine powder and mixed with egg yolk and then thinned with water. Tempera is capable of producing the translucent effects of light. Wyeth learned to use tempera from his brother-in-law Peter Hurd, an artist who also studied with N.C. Wyeth.

Andrew Wyeth and his wife Betsy still live in Chadds Ford in an eighteenth-century fieldstone building near the Brandywine River. During the Revolutionary War English troops were stationed close by. Twenty miles away the Americans positioned themselves at Valley Forge. This is where the famous battle of Brandywine occurred and the battlefield is now open to visitors. The Chadds Ford Inn is where Route 100 meets Route 1, having opened for business in 1736 as the Chadds Ford Hotel, a rest stop on the Wilmington-Philadelphia-Lancaster commerce routes. The food served there is reflective of the art of "sophisticated-simple" and authentic. The Christian Sanderson Museum at Chadds Ford is the prior eight-room home of Christian

Sanderson, who died in 1966. The Museum is filled with art, memorabilia, artifacts and curiosities some which relate to the Battle of Brandywine.

Andrew Wyeth was brought up "breathing art." The remarkable portraits of Christina Olson, until her death in 1967, began with *Christina Olson* in 1947 and *Christina's World* in 1948. The latter painting is somewhat startling with Christina, seen from behind, twisted awkwardly in the grass. She is focused on the house, severely crippled and proceeding to drag herself forward using her arms. This painting expresses the tragedy and joy of life that I have so often witnessed in the consultation room of my office. Perhaps this painting is appealing because it is the universal symbol of the human condition. It is easy for a doctor to identify with the painting. Christina's movements are with such difficulty that it is obvious this is her total world.

In 1952, Wyeth painted *Miss Olson*—Christina holding a sick kitten. The painting is astonishing in its realism. As with all of Wyeth's subjects, they reach from his heart and extend to ours.

Wyeth said he began his art career "wild, free and even explosive...art was in the air." He was, and continues to be, much influenced by Shakespeare, but the most important influence in his work is his father. "You see my father got me to the point of realism.... I was seeking the realness, the real feeling of the subject, all the texture around it, everything involved with it, even the atmosphere of the very day in which the object happened to exist...the right push from my father who recognized that excitement I had within me.... I wasn't after an image of something or an illusion of something. I quite literally wanted to have...the real object itself, or at least primarily the real object and only a little illusion. It was, in a sense, an almost primitive point of view, somewhat similar to the works of the Italian primitives of the thirteenth and fourteenth centuries." Wyeth adds, "I don't think I ever achieved it—never will—but, anyway that was the search." The next step was to come alive with the object.

Wyeth started painting from life in his studio and from that point on trained himself. He speaks of the struggles he goes through in making a tempera painting. Walking or driving—living—he has a feeling, an idea sparked by an elusive something rushes to the studio and draws a line, rushes out and then goes back to see if he is still excited about the idea. More drawings are made, a stage of slight boredom, then doubt. More drawings and then maybe start of a picture. Is it worth developing? "I pull a mood from a painting rather than trying to strike or force something into it... A picture must be abstractly exciting before you get into the image."

Wyeth has preserved for us the memories of our land—our uniqueness as Americans, and the memories of our experiences. A normal man, free of masks, he paints the truth of our soul. He is free to let things happen and to be *a part of* the things that are happening. His use of tempera involves the quality of the colors that simulate earth reality. Natural. "To me, it's like the dry mud of Brandywine Valley in certain times of the year or like these tawny fields that one can see outside my windows…the color I use is so much like the country I live in. Winter is that color here…it has a cocoon-like feeling of dry lostness—almost a lonely feeling." He speaks of the lasting quality of tempera "like an Egyptian mummy" and the need for arrangements for freedom of motion in a painting. Tempera is not for quick effect and the design must meet the needs for motion. Otherwise, watercolor or perhaps oil is the medium of choice.

Wyeth painted human beings in all aspects of their total environment. The subject is his "place," not the studio. He paints the life he experiences. The essential environments in his life have been the Kuerner's farm in Pennsylvania with its enduring quality and strength, and the Olson's place in Maine with its "spidery," "windy" quality providing the impression "...of crackling skeletons rattling in the attic." This is no studio, but "an environment"—a reality that allows Wyeth to become part of the total experience in both feeling and observation.

Wyeth visited the Olson's place on his twenty-second birthday when he met his wife, Betsy. He said that through the Olsons, he began to see New England as it really was and through the years was allowed free access in the Olson and Kuerner homes. This life became a natural extension of his life. "I didn't plan anything; it just happened." He eschewed the tradition of the studio and used the room and a sense of "sloppiness" to create. My studio is where I'm working.... It's part of my creativity. I don't think I exist really as a person, particularly. I really don't. And I'd rather not."

Objects in Wyeth's paintings become related to the spirit and the very essence of his subjects. Inanimate farm equipment takes on a life by association. The detail is crucial and "...abstracted through your vision." The use of detail is the method Wyeth uses to capture the *quality* of an object but he goes beyond realism to his own style of abstraction. Smell and sound are conveyed in color and line. The paintings "speak" to us. For example, in discussing *Spring Fed*, Wyeth talks about the water running, the hollow sound of the feet of cattle on the cement corral, and the shadows. "I think this picture has a lot of sound in it.... Everything is sound...that curious echo of things...like some sort of Egyptian tomb in Chadds Ford."

This simplicity is complex. In *Groundhog Day* (my favorite painting by *any* artist), Wyeth expresses the associations of the kitchen at the Kuerner farm—the light pouring in and all the feelings of a Pennsylvania

German farmhouse. "The whole country seems to hang on a pivot on that hub of a building." Many of Wyeth's works, such as *Pine Baron*, are symbolic of his creative process—finding the extraordinary in the ordinary, noticing the incongruous nature of the ordinary, and being surprised by it. The more you study an object, the more you see and the deeper it becomes emotionally. Like the book, *Wherever You Go, There You Are*, the emotional depth becomes reality.

Andrew Wyeth also interacted closely with his subjects, such as when he would wash Christina's face as it became dirty or when he would comb her hair. Thus, *Christina's World* becomes more than a portrait—it becomes her statement—her life—her existence. Christina was also a symbol of New England and Maine. "I'd think of that house sitting there and Christina down in that kitchen, *hearing in my mind* the sound of the lids of the stove rattling.... I'd hear the scraping of her chair.... It was *Maine*."

In *Weather Side*, Wyeth portrays the house as a universal object—looking deeply and penetratingly into and at it. Wyeth mentions something extremely important, a point that rings true: he is captivated and carried away by experiences that differ from place to place. "I don't think if you're truly emotional that you can concoct, truthfully anyway, the same set of values for one place as you can for another.... I think an artist should be a sounding board for all these nervous vibrations and should not just carry a set of rules and tricks around with him to use them on different objects." Wyeth speaks of this as being unemotional and lacking of true involvement. The feelings are, and must be different—Maine—Pennsylvania—are two different feeling worlds. It takes more than an art critic to understand this and Mark Rothko (chapter 4) seems to have been right in not trusting, believing in or liking such critics.

In 1986, Kathleen Jamieson, an interior decorator, told Penn-sylvania art collector Leonard Andrews about an exciting series of tempera paintings, watercolors and drawings Andrew Wyeth made between 1970 and 1985. As a result, Andrews drove out to the Wyeth place in Chadds Ford. At that time, Andrews already owned six Wyeths: a tempera, two drybrushes, and three watercolor drawings. When he discovered the "Helga Collection," Andrews was awestruck and realized he had come upon, in his words, "a national treasure." He purchased the entire collection of 240 drawings and paintings of Helga.

Betsy, Wyeth's wife, had *not known* of the full extent of the Helga works although she did have, in her living room, three of them: *Lovers, Night Shadow* and *Autumn.* Per agreement with Leonard Andrews, Betsy is to leave her three Helga paintings to the Leonard E. B. Andrews Foundation, the sponsor of the National Arts Program which encourages the development of indigenous artistic talent in America and provides scholarships and cash prizes for participating artists.

The entire Helga Collection is made up four tempera paintings, sixty-seven watercolors and the rest drawings. The Helga works were first displayed at the National Gallery of Art in Washington, D.C., eventually traveling throughout the United States and abroad. Simul-taneously, at the Corcoran Gallery, near the National Gallery, three generations of Wyeths were on exhibit: N.C., Andrew and Jamie.

Helga Testorf, a German woman, worked on the Kuerner farm. As a result of the hullabaloo about the subject, Wyeth's relationship with his model, and the alleged "secrecy" surrounding the works, Wyeth made the cover of both *Time* and *Newsweek* magazines in the same week in 1986 with the release and sale of the paintings. Helga, who was fifty-four at the time the paintings became known, but appeared much younger, remained discreet and silent, as did her daughter

Carmen, the subject of a few drawings. What is interesting about the series is the close attention by the artist of a model over an extended period of time—fifteen years—and the complexity of emotional depth of the works. The creation of mood is depicted in an elegant and yet evocative fashion. There are at least thirty interrelated poses—nude and clothed—indoors and out, asleep and awake, at various times and in different seasons. Some of the best works in the series are dry-brush watercolors with their rich and telling detail. Wyeth said he used dry-brush technique (wringing out the moisture from the brushes) when he became deeply emotionally involved with his subject.

The tempera works of Helga again bring the earth associations and the solidity of immediate experience—the "there you are" experience. We can project our feelings combining both our "identification" with the subject, Helga, and our association with the environment, the time and the mood—the romantic. We can identify with life in its utmost—feeling and reality. These are representations of American art—uniquely American in their multiple representations and style. This seems to trouble some critics who, after all, just talk and write. The human figure and the setting in Wyeth's art are typically American, as are the relaxed and natural poses. Wyeth shares these characteristics with the finest of American artists.

The final work in the Helga series is *Refuge*. Close to the earth, this dry-brush watercolor has been described by John Wilmerding of the National Gallery of Art in Washington as, "Not quite an image of tragic resignation, it is one of reserve and privacy...this one looks downward and inward."

I believe Thomas Hoving understated Wyeth when he described him as "one of America's most distinguished painters." Wyeth's works represent the very soul of America—the very meaning of the earth.

3

REMINISCING
IN TEMPO:
DUKE ELLINGTON

PART 1: MAGICAL THINGS—
THE INFLUENCE OF AFRICAN ART ON
WESTERN CIVILIZATION

> *Bill Moyers has recounted one of Joseph Campbell's favorite*
> *stories about an American delegate, a social philosopher, at*
> *an international conference on religion in Japan. He was*
> *heard to say to his Shinto Priest, "We've been now to a good*
> *many ceremonies and have seen quite a few of your shrines.*
> *But I don't get your ideology. I don't get your theology." The*
> *Japanese paused, as though in deep thought, and then*
> *slowly shook his head. "I think we don't have ideology," he*
> *said. "We don't have theology. We dance."*
>
> *– from The Power of Myth*

African music stands in contrast to European music in that the former is closely associated with daily life and the latter has relevance to special occasions. African music does not differentiate between music and dance and avoids the European habit of separating the two "as if one accompanied the other." The *sound* of the music is only one element in the experience which may include clothing, customs, physical sensations of dancing, and the feeling and warmth of others. The psychoanalyst Phyllis Rose discussed artistic creation as the restoration of the state in which one's sense of self is expanded in *fantasy* or fused with an external object. The "external object" is the *transitional object* discussed throughout this book by psychoanalyst D.W. Winnicott.

The "stand in" of the creative object or experience is a reflection of the earlier (developmental) experience of self and other-mother, and I and mother, as well as I and the outside world. Rose emphasizes that artistic creativity makes us of bodily activity, an assertion that is especially valid with regard to African dance musical performance. This perspective of African music helps us to understand that the earliest signs of artistic talent are most likely to be observed in the child's motor organization with, as described by Phyllis Rose, "...the temporary lifting of the boundaries between self and object" and the formal qualities of thought thus producing "an idealized representation of the workings of one's own mind." This is the freedom that Mark Rothko (chapter 4) sought and that Andrew Wyeth (chapter 1) found so easily.

Although somewhat paradoxical when one considers the large variety of musical instruments, "virtually all African music is conceived vocally." Many African instruments are used to imitate the human voice: the most famous of the "talking" instruments are the drums of West and Central African tribes. John Storm Roberts, author of *Black Music of Two Worlds,* wrote, "The principle and essential traits of African music, its melodic, harmonic and rhythmic characteristics, are all linked to the making of the essentially speaking instrument."

Roberts noted, "Jazz has been described as vocalized music. The heavy vibrato of African speech expressing itself in the overtones of great Negro players, the essentially singing qualities of soloists such as Louis Armstrong and Dodds being directly related to the lines of voice." Duke Ellington's distinct contribution to music has been his development of a style of brass playing that has close semblance to the great blues shouters, while the brass effects have been referred to as the "growl" or "jungle" style. The term "jungle," however, is an inappropriate characterization of the music implying primitive or barbaric behaviors.

These terms were used for publicity when the Ellington band was trying to make a name for itself in New York. The "growl" is but one facet of a selection of mute, plunger and bowler effects made famous by James "Bubber" Miley who replaced Arthur Whetsol in the early Washingtonian Band of Ellington. Miley dramatically altered the sound of the orchestra and became a major instrumentalist. His importance extended to moving the Ellington band in the direction of New Orleans style Jazz and he used wah-wah mutes simulating the human voice and thus the African style of combining speech and song. The music historian John Hasse noted that Miley helped "define an Ellington sound." He was replaced in 1929 by Charles "Cootie" Williams who used the growl and plunger technique, expanding the music's emotional range. Williams spent twenty-three years with the Ellington band.

Although blended with the American culture, Negro music is essentially an expression of African civilization modified by Western values resulting in a perception of who the Negro thinks he is (has been) in America, what he would like to be, and his aspirations for acculturation, identification or rejection of the existing culture. This varies from region to region and time to time. Negro music in America is thus an expression of the adaptation and acculturation of Black peoples in a predominantly white society.

In slave quarters there were two parties, "the dancing party" and the "praying party." On holidays, the dancing party, commanding the allegiance of the bulk of the slaves, was responsible for entertainment and something beyond mere entertainment, the expression of "the existential absurdity" of their existence. The praying party, whose day was Sunday, perpetuated the sense of obedience and an adherence to Christianity, much of it proselytized by white interpretive versions. The chain gangs, a parallel of the persecutions of the Middle Ages and the concentration (death) camps of Nazi Germany, contributed in a major way to the flowering of Black music in America. This music became a melding of African, European and American elements—spirituals, work songs, "devil songs," funeral dirges and hymns. It was Bessie Smith, born impoverished in Tennessee, who went out into the world and sang the blues. It is important to note the parallel development of African-American music and the civil rights movement in America and the contributions each made to the other.

The importance of the development of rhythm from Africa is related to the syncopations in the music as they are expressed in both the spiritual and the work songs.

The minstrels of the South essentially prepared the way for the acceptance of Negro music which initially involved imitation and ridicule of Blacks and then, eventually ridicule of whites. The so-called "Coon Songs" are an example, representing the Black social prejudice and predicament of the late 1880s. "Cake-walks" were a syncopated dance characterized by high kicking and prancing which represented a "takeoff" of the manners and behavior of "the white folk" in the plantation houses. The expression "that takes the cake" is likely derived from this social dance behavior, representing an imitation of the social life of the plantation. The lyrics of the Coon Songs were atrocious, such as "all coons look alike for me" and some of the record albums of the time depict watermelons, chickens and razors on their covers, representative of the stereotyping and prejudice of the day.

The *ragtime* music of the day developed around the river cities of New Orleans and Chicago and is considered original by music historians, perhaps in great part because of its syncopation. Original means new, creative—something that did not exist before. Scott Joplin, who developed much of this music, was original regarding both the use of syncopation as well as his unique compositions. Negro music was considered the "life blood" of Southern Blacks and a method of communication both collectively and individually. While initially drums were used for music, they were soon outlawed because they were a means of communication between Blacks on different plantations. Thus developed the hand clapping and heel tapping that became important in the evolution of Black music, both socially and in the religious activities of the churches.

Prior to the Civil War, separate Black churches were outlawed but there were separate seats for whites and Blacks. For instance, the back and upper levels were reserved only for Blacks. Sometimes there were separate services in the same church. When Blacks established their own churches, much to the consternation of white people, they were met with contempt and hostility. The foot tapping and hand clapping was integrated into the music of the church and became essential to Black musical expression, eventually finding its way to Ragtime and Jazz.

Duke Ellington was well aware of Black history. He had 800 volumes of books on Black history, many of which he studied and underlined, especially the sections dealing with slave rebellions. His expression of racial concerns was subtle and creative. Scott Joplin was exposed to this milieu of early Black experience in music as contrasted with Ellington who was exposed to the so-called "more mature" Victorian music, a result of his mother's influence and direction. Thus the compositions of these two great Black composers had very separate development. Ellington and Joplin both shared the desire to be "serious" musicians. Joplin, however, eventually composed what is regarded as the first American opera *Tremonisha,* while Ellington regarded himself as having two careers: band leader *and* composer, and he did not want them confused.

Ellington was able to use the African derivatives of music in early Jazz, especially incorporating a technique called *heterophony* in which secondary voices sing variations of the melody and harmonize with it in only an approximate fashion. Jazz goes back to the turn of the century and is a Negro invention—music with an African foundation developing in an American environment. The entire field of rhythmic dance music is thrown together into what is termed Jazz. Hot Jazz (as contrasted with modern and symphonic) can be said to relate to the dance music of New Orleans Negroes and the white groups in Chicago that copied their ideas. The art of improvising on a theme goes back to the Negro bands of street parades.

The basis of Jazz is found in a strong underlying and steady rhythm, the imagination of individual performers using the melody as a point of departure to improvise and the performer's virtuosity on his given instrument. (Ellington made strong distinctions between spontaneous and more composed Jazz arrangements, fre-quently developing pieces that sounded spontaneous but were written and planned well in advance). Jazz may be considered dance music in duple meter with the frequent use of syncopation. Most importantly, Jazz represents a *freedom of expression.*

In her article "Jazz Cleopatra," Phyllis Rose discusses the life of Josephine Baker and the Revue Negre in Paris. She mentions the "litmus test for racial attitudes," and more importantly, gives us a substantial glimpse into the impact of African art and culture on Western civilization and creativity. For example, she discusses Pablo Picasso's visit to the Muse de Sculpture Comparee while looking for inspiration. Although Picasso had seen African masks and figures before, he followed the suggestion of a friend and took a look at the African pieces in the Musee Ethnographique. The pieces were not tastefully displayed nor assembled with any particular relevance and he noted, "It was disgusting, a flea market...the smell...I wanted to get out of there. I didn't leave. I stayed."

Picasso sensed something unusual happening. "He realized why he was a painter; not to represent the world, but to evoke and deflect psychological forces, spirits, to enchant, release, be a priest, perform exorcisms. *The African masks were tools and weapons with which man waged his war on demons within and without: Magical things.* They mediated and interceded between man and the forces of evil."

For a time it was thought Picasso was incorporating into his painting a formal tribute to African sculpture, but, more recently, people have begun to realize that African masks were painted by him "for their emotional impact, to express the terrifying aspects of female sexuality." While Phyllis Rose refers to Picasso's painting *Les Demoiselle,* she states his belief that African masks would arouse terror in everyone depended on a long European tradition associating the African with the terrifying. "More specifically, he was calling upon the association between female sexuality and Blackness which only exists from the white perspective. He had alluded to it before...female sexuality and the Black were, for Picasso, visual analogies."

Josephine Baker's presentation in the Paris of the Twenties was, as Phyllis Rose terms it, "not ideological artifact. The enthusiasm wasn't just for art; *it was for race"* (emphasis added). This is similar to the Renaissance societies when Blacks were a rarity in Europe, and therefore valued and frequently kept in residence in the courts, somewhat like pets.

The *magic* is still with us!

PART 2: A DIPLOMAT AMONG ARTISTS— THE SYMPHONY OF CREATIVITY

Edward Kennedy Ellington was born April 29, 1899 in Washington D.C. He married Edna Thompson, pregnant with his son Mercer, on July 2, 1918. Mercer was born March 11, 1919. Ellington's closest confidants in life were his mother Daisy, his physician Arthur C. Logan, with whom he forged a close relationship after his mother's death in 1935, and Billy Strayhorn, Ellington's arranger, pianist and assistant. Dr. Logan was also physician to Martin Luther King, Jr.

Billy Strayhorn, "Sweet Pea" or "Strays" as he was called, was practically the opposite of Ellington in lifestyle and physical appearance. He was also homosexual. However, Ellington said that with Strays he was so close their brain waves meshed.

Duke Ellington died in 1974 at the age of 75, leaving more than 3000 compositions. In the 1920s he led a band of individualists. During the 1930s he rose in stature as a composer concerned with harmony and form and their integration with Jazz. In the 1940s and 1950s, Ellington's musical patterns became innovative and perhaps somewhat simpler as he preserved a strong central identity. He produced such diverse "civil rights" pieces as *King Fit The Battle of Alabam* and *My People,* and wrote the underscore—background—music for *Timon of Athens* at the Shakespeare Festival in Stratford, Ontario. During the late 1950s and 1960s his musical vision and creativity broadened to include such works as the *Concert of Sacred Music* and *The Queen's Suite,* dedicated to Queen Elizabeth.

Duke Ellington has been described as having charisma from childhood through the end of his life, possessing a majesty that was simultaneously unique and utilitarian. His character and his talent were said to have been one. As Joseph Campbell would say, Ellington was a typical hero who has given his life to something larger than himself and other than himself in a transformation of consciousness. Ellington communicated to our unconscious mind in the context of his music. At his death in 1974 he left "one of the most significant bodies of music of the 20th century."

During his fifty-year career, Ellington played at over 20,000 per-formances in the United States, Europe, the Middle East and Latin America and had reached tens of millions of people. In 1988 and 1991, the Smithsonian acquired 200,000 pages of documents, half of which are music scores, about 500 objects such as plaques and medals, and a host of unpublished music manuscripts. Also included are two thousand photographs, records and related items. This has all become part of the Smithsonian exhibition *Beyond Category: The Musical Genius of Duke Ellington* touring the United States contemporaneously as I write this book. This work was carved, as James Collier noted, with the "chisel of his character."

James Collier, a music historian and author, stated that in America the end result of Black culture was "a subculture spread through the social body that was neither entirely of it nor entirely out of it. American

Blacks existed in a side culture running parallel to the mainstream, very similar to, and at times joining, but never entirely part of the central culture. On the one hand, we have had the attempts of Blacks to acculturate in the American society, to make identifications and to obtain the advantages whites possess. On the other hand, we have a rejection of a culture that has presented major obstacles to acculturation." In the wake of this confrontation, a style of entertainment developed that was major influence on the evolution of Black music and the expression of the genius of Duke Ellington.

Ellington emulated a white culture that espoused Victorian values, an interest in the arts, a formal manner of dress, deportment and speech, and, above all, an optimism and belief in achievement. His parents lived with the ideal of Victorian gentility until they died, and they raised their son accordingly. Collier noted in 1987 that Duke Ellington was "part of a social group whose members have risen to genuine achievements and were vested with pride and a sense of superiority, not merely over "lower" Blacks, but over a good many whites as well."

Long before the "Black is Beautiful Movement," Ellington's racial pride, his good manners, character that demanded respect, his grace and his tolerance were all evident. His father, James Edward (known as "J.E."), was a chauffeur and later a butler for a prominent Washington physician, Middleton F. Cuthbert. Although he had not completed the eight grade, J.E. got along well with the doctor.

J.E. migrated north from North Carolina and saw himself in an aristocratic light, passing this trait on to his children. Ellington identified with this characteristic of his father, which was reinforced by his mother. Throughout his life Ellington insisted on going "first class" and judged himself on the basis of style. His mother, Daisy Kennedy, grew up with similar Victorian views and a religious orientation. As Ruth, Ellington's sister, once said, "My mother was quite puritanical. A real Victorian lady."

Ellington was likely his mother's *replacement child*. Sister Ruth was born when he was sixteen and yet his birth certificate specifies that he was the second child born to Daisy and James Ellington. Duke Ellington shared this characteristic with Vincent Van Gogh (chapter 8), although with a much different personality outcome.

A characteristic finding in such a replacement child situation is an over-determined love relationship between mother and child and a doting mother throughout a lifetime relationship. This was certainly true for Duke Ellington. As Freud once stated, "A man who has been the indisputable favorite of his mother keeps for life the feeling of a conqueror, that confidence of success that often induces real success." Whatever the reasons, Ellington's development was characterized by the exclusive doting of his mother and a sense of aristocracy that remained with him until his death. He was an only child until near adulthood. The name he adopted, "Duke," relies on both the attribution of aristocracy and the expectation of how he was to be treated by others. He remained aristocratic in bearing and behaviors his entire life. Part of this related to being taught pride in his race and a "responsibility" to represent it well. Positive aspects of race were emphasized in his home. Ellington said that his friend Edgar McEntree nicknamed him "Duke" in response to these qualities.

Although his parents struggled financially, Ellington's childhood was comfortable and likely happier than most. He was a well-loved member of a large extended family and the recipient of extraordinary attention by his mother, whom, he once said, "never took her eyes off precious little me, her jewel, until I was four years old...." Ellington was given the sense that he was special and was actually told by his mother that he was "blessed"—this clearly meant that he was beyond the ordinary. His perception forged a significant part of his character throughout his life. On one occasion he autographed a photo of himself to give to his mother signed, "To the dearest mother in the whole world, from Edward." The availability of a warmly supportive parent has particular importance to creativity in adult life and also provides for inner stability in times of creative and non-creative crises.

Psychoanalyst Phyllis Greenacre discussed the phenomena in which creative people are protected against disappointments in adolescence and early adult life, particularly as it relates to disillusionment of their parents and the success in finding ego ideals. Ellington was certainly able to find mentors such as Doc Perry and Henry Grant whom he could look up to. He was free to form positive relationships without the fear of disillusionment. Such people are, according to Greenacre, protected against their disappointments by "a love affair with the world." They are the individuals with the ability to erect "creative alternatives." Gifted children are also likely to respond with compensatory fantasies of exalted parentage. In Ellington's circumstance, we find the aristocracy that was so easily appropriated from both parents, a sense of nobility that he carried with him throughout his life, and a lifelong attachment to his mother. Psychoanalyst Ernst Kris presents evidence in his book *The Personal Myth* that, in the process of disavowing the significance of certain pathological aspects of one's character, one espouses a certain primitive romantic idealization. Life becomes and remains beautiful and hopeful.

The issue of the *replacement child syndrome* is another matter altogether. Vincent Van Gogh was a replacement for his name's sake, a brother who died a year preceding his birth. Van Gogh's mother was still in mourning at the time of the second child's birth and Vincent Van

Gogh's own later relationships in adult life are a reflection of the consequences of this kind of tragic beginning. He had feelings of emptiness and of being "ghostlike" when his adult relationships did not maintain themselves in accordance with his dependent and demanding needs. Van Gogh's situation differs from Ellington's in that Van Gogh's repetitive depressive episodes also resulted from an early milieu (unlike Ellington's experience), as Van Gogh's mother had severe psychological disturbances including depression. Four of her six children grew up with severe psychological problems. Ellington's mother, in contrast, was optimistic, creative and strong-willed. Also in Ellington's case the replacement syndrome worked in the direction of advantage—creatively and professionally. The close attachment with his mother, however, likely created problems of intimacy in his heterosexual relationships as well as contributing to his sexual adventures—of which there were many.

When Ellington's mother, Daisy, was sent to Providence Hospital in Detroit in May 1935, Ellington spent the last three days of her life with his head on her pillow. She died on May 27. He was devastated; his mother had been the center of his emotional life. He had chosen to live with her for a substantial portion of his adult life and, in many respects, had replaced his father in family relationships and as head of the household. Ellington became the provider, bearer of expensive clothing, sole source of his mother's social status and center of importance. His world was built around his mother. Her loss from cancer was followed by Ellington's depression, heavy drinking and lack of productivity. He wrote, "After my mother passed, there was really nothing, and my sparkling parade was probably at an end." He never fully recovered from this loss which was reinforced by later losses, the greatest of which was Strayhorn's death.

The loss of Ellington's mother was the saddest period of his life and he had actually cut down on his work the month prior to her passing. Eventually his suffering was reduced to an anniversary reaction, during which time he would drink heavily. The drunk would last two or three weeks and then gradually subside. Each year he would lose his ambition for living for a time and the repetitive loss affected his musical output more than anything else in his career.

Similar in behavior to Scott Joplin who composed *Tremonisha* while mourning the loss of his daughter, Ellington finally broke out of his slump and composed *Reminiscing in Tempo,* a quiet melancholy tone poem in which he experimented with more advanced harmonies. He moved beyond the expected category of Jazz to express strong emotion. Vic Bellerby, author of *Duke Ellington: The Art of Jazz, Ragtime to Be-Bop* wrote, "His dreamy impressionism is most exacting in its demands of the technical proficiency and tonal blending of his musicians." Ellington said that the manuscript was stained with his tears. It was his longest composition to date (moving forward in the commercial realm) and the most complex work yet with asymmetrical phrase lengths. The creative product grew out of his grieving experience.

Reminiscing in Tempo was a four-part recording in which his mood alternated from the sadness of the past shared with his mother, to fond memories—clearly a reaction to her death. This work was different from his previous music and was not well received by critics. It stands as an indication of the re-emergence of his creative thinking and a paradigm of his genius. It is a *creative alternative* to grief. There were also practical considerations along with his despair when one considers the medical bills he had to pay for both his mother and father. His father, J.E., died in Columbia Presbyterian Hospital October 28, 1937.

The most disappointing years of his career were 1935 and 1936. Not only did he produce fewer records, but the ones he did make were of decidedly inferior quality, especially compared with his previous work. He had new competitors, his friend Artie Whetsol was seriously ill, he was grieving the loss of his mother, and the music "market" was changing.

Not long after his mother's death, Ellington, in 1937, formed a friendship with Arthur C. Logan, a prominent Black physician. Logan, perhaps more than anyone else, was to become Ellington's confidant and one of the most important people in his life. After significant emotional loss some creative individuals form a new intense relationship that lasts indefinitely and with whom they closely identify. They "fill in" the emotional space. Interestingly, this emotional intensity appears to have been missing in Ellington's relationship with his son, Mercer.

Mercer, in his biography, explains a different aspect of the relationship between father and son and describes himself as being his father's alter ego. To some extent this was a position each shared for the other but Ellington appears to have "used" Mercer and saw his son's life as an extension of his own. Mercer, in describing the negative aspects of the relationship, discusses hate as being "such a luxurious emotion, it can only be spent on ones we love deeply." His book provides a much more balanced view of the relationship between father and son than the books of other music historians and critics. After all, Mercer knew him intimately.

In the biographies of great men, it is startling to find the dependence on a benign father figure. Even Freud had Wilhelm Fliess. Early on, Ellington's relationship with his agent, Irving Mills, served this purpose and there is evidence that they collaborated on many of the compositions. Mills earned a great deal of money from Ellington, and recognized his penchant to go "First Class." Ellington, in turn, recognized the importance of Mills in his life and always spoke highly of him. Mills' role was later supplanted by Arthur C. Logan in a much more intimate and trusting way.

Identification with the activities of males is noted quite early in the development of heterosexual men and is reinforced in later childhood and adolescence. Ellington's father was rather passive and, in later life, Duke Ellington became a father to his own father, providing financial and emotional resources which ultimately led to the destruction of the senior Ellington. Duke Ellington's identification with his mother allowed him an opportunity to deal with unconscious procreative wishes ordinarily repressed in the male. He had the best of both worlds and was able to relate, form close relationships, and lead men.

Phyllis Greenacre asserted the hypothesis that major artistic, as well as other creativity, is the collate of childlessness. Ellington's attempt to deny, or at least to avoid, the existence of his son during the latter's formative years is well noted. This contributed to an intense focus on the creative aspect of his work. A similar example is that of Van Gogh who spoke of his paintings as his children—produced with his brother Theo.

Psychoanalyst John E. Gedo wrote that the key to understanding men of genius is the "inevitable underestimation that typified their formative years." This situation gives forth their need to create and a fragile sense of self-worth. That is, the deeply rooted sense of identification. Other personality traits are then influenced by other childhood experiences. Ellington's overemphasis of "going First Class" and his need to maintain control and complete esteem in the eyes of others is an important defensive characteristic in maintaining his own inner self-esteem. He had to be in control of everything even when he wasn't.

The *reaction formation*, which he used to deal with his aggression, served a similar function. Ellington's autobiography is almost entirely positive about every person he met. There is barely a negative comment in the entire book. Ernst Kris called attention to the distorting effects of standard biographies of artists, applying idealizing formulas that conceal the actual facts. This is always a problem in attempting to reconstruct the psychological life of an individual, and in gaining an understanding of the repetition compulsion of childhood transaction with caretakers, especially the mother-child relationship, and later developmental experiences that lead to either creative endowment or neurotic inhibition.

Because the adoption of Victorian attitudes and standards of the white culture were an important part of upward mobility, it is understandable that Blacks in this socioeconomic category would "disassociate themselves from Ragtime music, the early vestiges of Jazz, the Trots, the Blues, and similar manifestations of the 1920s Jazz age" according to Vic Bellerby. Indeed, the word Jazz was frequently synonymous with sex. Ellington's grandparents were, doubtless, no strangers to the chain gangs and violence of the late 1880s, including lynchings, and it's not surprising that the family espoused the desire to distance themselves from any aspect of amoral and uneducated behavior. In a sense, they were *identifying with the aggressor* in white society.

Duke Ellington grew up in the European musical tradition and likely knew very little of Black folk music. During early development he showed very little musical talent, wasn't interested in learning music, and was not a good student when his mother attempted to arrange piano lessons for him at age 8 or 9. One important permanent personality characteristic of his life was his resistance to formal study.

He had problems in following through with discipline and was not responsive to direction. As Sonny Greer, his drummer and confidant, once said, "Duke would never ask you to show him something; no, his pride wouldn't allow that." Ellington himself once said, "I can never catch on to whatever anyone else played, so I developed my own stuff." His lack of skill forced him to invent ways to get around deficits and it fostered a creativity that might have otherwise not developed. He learned to organize his music according to his own instinct.

Musicologists frequently discuss his greatest strength—"the tone palette"—that was recognized early on as commendable. Never has any Jazz composer been able to sound out such completely different moods as Ellington. Although referred to as "improvised" music, many of the greatest Jazz pieces owe their apparent spontaneity to detached preparation by this strong composer. He was an expert at preparing compositions that sounded improvised.

Ellington was of such singular purpose in influencing his soloists that their improvisations were a logical function of a greater unity. The work is a result of years of experimentation and the development of collective understanding. Ellington had a deep love of *color* for its own sake and could often deliberately disregard melody and rhythm for harmonic development. Subtle harmonic changes would create a dreamy effect, suspending the music in space. His personal influence is in each and every composition and tune. As with his clothing and conversation, Duke Ellington created his own musical style by innovation and rule breaking. He maintained a give-and-take policy with his musicians and avoided "stock" presentations. He worked *with* his instrumentalists, not at them.

Mercer mentions his father's early artistic tendencies in high school and particularly that his paintings attracted attention. He notes that with Ellington, it was not only the music but the life that attracted him, particularly when women and others paid attention to him. Music for Ellington, at least in the early days, was a way of earning a living, meeting women and being part of the good times. Like Mark Rothko, who fortuitously discovered the world of painting nudes, Ellington discovered the world of music and they both became serious artists. Mercer also emphasizes that the Duke never really wanted the role of parent which Mercer thought had to do with Ellington's defense against getting old. Mercer was even instructed to refer to his grandparents as "aunt" and "uncle." It was probably painful for Mercer to recognize that his father really wanted a female child.

As a result of Ellington's lack of ability to read music and his educational deficits, he "did it by ear." He would figure out what someone else had done by listening to the beat and analyzing it. No one fully understands how Ellington accomplished this. Mercer emphasizes that throughout his father's entire life he had a disdain for formalized training and, even when given honorary doctorates, still had the feeling that the concept of a scholar was something false. Mercer notes that his father was "…different from the beginning. He sought a sensuality in the way his music was expressed: There was always an emotion attached to the sound."

Ellington was highly conscious of the need to make the listener feel experiences with sound, as if he were creating apparitions within the music. For example, *Sophisticated Lady,* according to Mercer, related to Mercer's mother Edna, her depressed state of mind and consequent drinking after the marital breakup. *Black and Tan Fantasy* commemorated the death of love and the end of Ellington's affair with an actress. Some say this piece was largely written by Miley, whose solo ranks as one of the greatest plunger-mute solos ever recorded.

The piece remained in the Ellington repertoire throughout his career and was also a feature of a nineteen-minute movie *Black and Tan* made in 1927.

Ellington never graduated from high school because his wife-to-be, Edna, became pregnant. With the doors to the professions closed to gifted and intelligent Blacks, he turned to what was virtually his only choice—music. The entertainment industry became the vanguard of the integration movement in the United States. Eventually Ellington became part of the Harlem Renaissance where Black artists, writers and thinkers came to develop themselves and produce at the cutting edge of musical creativity. John Hasse writes that Ellington "must be seen as a key figure of the cultural awakening of Harlem. He would achieve as much as any literary figure of the Renaissance, and would keep on achieving after most of the writers had faded or died." He notes that Ellington is given little role in this awakening because literary and cultural historians are unprepared to assess music and its cultural impact and importance. "In the Black community, music reached more people than did literature."

Ellington was proud of his heritage and, although he initially ignored racial problems, he composed a great number of pieces celebrating Black culture and was well aware of the unequal and denigrating status of Black Americans. He had definite ideas about the racial problems in the United States but preferred to be subtle and make his statements artistically. Once, when asked about the discrimination and prejudice he experienced he responded, "I took the energy it takes to pout and wrote some blues." Another example of a creative alternative.

Ruth, Ellington's sister, had been criticized for having had a "complex about whites," because her first two husbands were white, because she wore a blonde wig, and because she associated with whites. Her behavior and attitude reflected the Ellington attitude that they were as good as most whites and better than many.

Ellington's early experiences in a pool hall taught him how to deal with people and how to manipulate. He was one of the all-time masters at pool. Later in his career he placed expensive ads in trade magazines so the columnists wouldn't write anything bad about him for fear of losing a good client. The manner in which Ellington conducted himself in style of dress, language and behavior as well as, and perhaps as much as, his creativity, gave African-Americans someone to look up to. This handsome, elegant, graceful, sophisticated artist made his statement by his very being. His contributions to the Harlem Renaissance were of enormous significance in the emergence of Black energy in the expression of Black culture.

While Duke Ellington gradually developed his interest in Black culture and the themes of Black life relatively early in his career, by 1927 we find specific energy in this direction. During his first Cotton Club Review in 1927 he wrote the song *Black Beauty,* the first of a long series of musical portraits. It was dedicated to the memory of Florence Mills, the singer/dancer who died at age thirty-two. Her Harlem funeral was attended by 150,000 people. John Hasse describes the song as one of the "orchestra's most resplendent compositions." This piece is an example of Ellington's tendency to write consecutive rather than repetitive melody, producing the effect of speech or dialogue, once again consistent with African musical inclination and not likely a product of his early childhood music exposure.

One perspective of Ellington's attitude toward racial problems was to *not* focus on them. He was certainly aware of the problems and did what he could under the circumstances by hiring Black musicians, having a preference for Blacks in his band, and by presenting his own image of musical integrity, elegance and sophistication. He did not lower himself by engaging in the arguments and the confrontive taunts of the day. It is very much to his credit and honor that he did not speak poorly of a country and a people who treated Blacks so badly.

Without question, Ellington enjoyed a far greater acceptance in white society than most Blacks. He eventually became a spokesman for Jazz and for his race, but not without significant criticism from political figures such as Adam Clayton Powell. On the other hand, Martin Luther King, Jr. was more understanding of Ellington's situation and appreciated his efforts. We will never know how much internal conflict Duke Ellington experienced in expressing the music of his heart because even his family and members of the Black community of his origin had strong opposition to popular music, especially the Blues. They saw this music as a product of the devil and, in any case, not a mark of distinction for upwardly mobile Blacks.

When asked by Edmund Anderson what he considered a typical Negro piece among those he had written, to Anderson's surprise Ellington suggested *In A Sentimental Mood.* Anderson said he thought it was a sophisticated "white kind" of a song and that people were surprised Ellington had written the music (lyrics were actually added by Manny Kurtz and Irving Mills.) Ellington's response was dramatic, "That's because you don't know what it's like to be a Negro." This piece of sophisticated melancholy was not far from Ellington's character.

An "All Negro Review" in 1941 is one example of Ellington's attempt to portray the history of his race in a show of "social significance" for which Americans of the time were not yet ready. In his autobiography, Ellington portrays *Jump For Joy* as a success—but it hardly was so. This program attempted to deal with Black stereotyping by presenting a history of the Negro in America. It was the first major musical to attempt to portray Blacks realistically and offered an opportunity for a source of pride for African-Americans. It opened in Los Angeles but never made it to Broadway, a circumstance that remained a great disappointment for Ellington throughout his life.

A more recent study of this work reveals the complicated composition style of Ellington and his tendency to rearrange passages until he found the sound he wanted. Ellington was not successful with his major concert pieces. Music critics found them to be much too rambling, lacking in coordination and without structure. This may be because of his use of fragmentation devices and thematic recall in depicting the lives of African-Americans.

Black, Brown and Beige is one such concert which attempts to portray the lives of Black Americans and their integration into the "collateral culture" of America. It debuted at Carnegie Hall in January 1943 and was a financial success but received negative reviews—possibly because of the issues associated with Black history and problems in fully understanding the work from this perspective. Ellington was very discouraged about this extended composition which was, after all, a civil rights statement. He was offering Black history and social criticism in a very subtle and constructive way. Characteristically, he used some of this music in a later production called *My People*. Part of the difficulty with the concert pieces was Ellington's belief that literary parallel would hold the music together. He did not fully realize the music would have to sustain itself in musical terms.

Ellington was much more successful with the early 1940 recording of *Ko-Ko* as a reflection of African tribal music in a harmoniously sophisticated way. *Ko-Ko* uses the technique of holding a note continuously, a technique known as *pedal* to musicians. This is a dramatic piece that builds in intensity. *Harlem Airshaft* (July 1940) is another success story triggered by the memory of an airshaft in a Harlem tenement building.

Ellington had a taste for trained voices such as those found at concerts put on by Black musical organizations. The concerts had been part of the social life of upper and middle class Blacks when he was growing up and he tended to use such singers rather than some of the more popular Jazz singers of the day. One possible exception was Ivie Anderson whose excellent diction and relaxed sensitivity is well noted. Quite versatile, she remained with the orchestra for eleven years.

Duke Ellington represented the United States well in his travels and shrewdly dealt with Communists who attempted to bait him about civil rights injustices in the United States. They wanted criticism of the white power structure in America, but Ellington did not allow himself to be used or manipulated. He also understood that the battle with race and color was not limited to the United States. He knew many facts about Blacks that others would not wish to know or remember, such as their involvement in the institution of slavery in Africa and their profits from the sale of slaves to the Dutch, Portuguese and English. He was also highly cognizant of the positive contributions Blacks had made in the United States.

In his biography of his father, Mercer discusses the development of his father's awareness of Black pride and his evolutionary involvement. He quotes Ellington as saying, "I think a statement of social protest in the theatre should be made without saying it." This was Ellington's attempt in *Jump For Joy* and similar pieces. In *Black, Brown and Beige,* he had much to say about the Black contribution to American history but had to withstand criticism from both sides—white and Black—in these situations. One thing he would not discuss in an interview was racial issues.

Although Ellington's book *Music Is My Mistress,* published in 1973, is a description of his career and love for music, it is hardly an apt description of his love life. In fact, he doesn't even mention the names of the important women in his life. This book can hardly be called an autobiography and remarkably does not deal with "unpleasant" or private issues. Although he remained ever "loyal" to his wife, Edna, he took Mildred Dixon, a dancer, to be his partner in 1929 after his move to an apartment in the fancy Sugar Hill area of Harlem. Mercer came home from school one day "and there was a strange woman living with my father and taking care of me and Ruth." Characteristically, Ellington did not want to deal with the "negatives." He remained on "friendly terms" with Edna, and never divorced her. He also convinced his mother and father to come live with him, Mercer and Ruth in New York. One can only speculate whether this was an expression of creative genius, emotional freedom, the behavior of an artist very much in charge of his life and decision making, or an example of psychopathology—the distancing of intimacy. In all of this there is a need to control, to dominate those around him and intense loyalty and protectiveness of those individuals intimately related to him—whether family or fellow artists. This is all characteristic Ellington.

The treatment of his son Mercer, is even more restrictive. He regarded Mercer as a potential rival and the symbolic "castration" is clearly evident. Mercer's hair was kept in braids for years so his father would tolerate his presence. In his autobiography, Ellington begins his description of his son with the phrase, "My son, Mercer Ellington, is dedicated to maintaining the luster of his father's image." In his own book, Mercer wrote about the "cold war" relationship he had with his father.

Duke Ellington appears to have changed significant heterosexual partners approximately every ten years. He married Edna in 1917, began living with Mildred Dixon in 1929, took up with "Edie" (Beatrix Ellis) in 1939 and sometime later became involved with a woman Mercer describes as "a dancer." When he went off with Edie, he left Mercer with Mildred Dixon. Ellington's sexual appetite seems to have been insatiable and there were numerous affairs with girlfriends of members of the band, as well as with acquaintances. He stated that women were the initial reason for his attraction and dedication to music. Perhaps he never divorced Edna so he could use this as an excuse to never marry anyone else. To the end of his days his devotion remained to his mother, the most important woman in his life and somehow Ellington was also able to keep his private life out of the newspapers.

In 1959 Ellington began an affair with Fernanda de Castro Monte, a Caucasian woman known as Madam Zajj. She was twenty years younger than he was, a striking blonde and spoke five languages. The relationship began when the band was playing in Las Vegas and appears to be his last deep relationship. Madam Zajj's main interest was art. She also had considerable interest in music and she traveled with him and influenced him strongly in cultural matters. Mercer comments that his father "disappeared" and was engulfed by Zajj; "That she constructed a kind of fortress for him at El Rancho Vegas was evident." He also states that she had a positive and constructive influence on his father. Unlike other women who paid him attention "...she never hesitated to voice criticism when she felt it was called for. Prior to this he had reached a kind of creative plateau but in her he now found the inspiration to create anew."

The many flirtations and light affairs did not influence Ellington's life as much as these four women did. (Mercer mentions there were five.) Significantly, Mercer also notes that his father "never seemed to be interested in the perfect woman." He looked for women with a basic flaw, such as a scar or a slight disproportion in her body.

Marriages of band members broke up because of Ellington and there were at least five instances of members of the band who met and married women with whom Ellington had affairs. Band members may have seen themselves as extensions of Ellington, relating to him by becoming involved with these women. Surprisingly, Mercer writes, "I would say that apart from his mother and sister, he had a basic contempt for women." He further notes, "He spent so much time celebrating and charming them, but basically hated them. In many cases, once he uncovered a weakness, or brought them to heel, so to speak, he passed them on to someone else; but it was a love-hate thing actually, and more hate than love." Mercer cites lyrics his father wrote indicative of this perspective toward women such as in the song: *She Always Wanted to be a Witch.*

Mercer mentions only two women in Ellington's life to whom he responded on a basic level—his mother and his sister, Ruth. To some extent Ellington "relived" his relationship with his mother in the presence of her sister Flossie, who was similar to Daisy in appearance and manner. Ellington took care of his aunt, seeing his own mother in her image. According to Mercer, "He even thought of Ruth as the image of his mother, as this was the one big feeling he had, the focal point of emotion and attention. His feeling for his mother was akin to religion in that it had to do with the guiding light between right and wrong, an element that stabilized or determined what was to be his mission. The ethereal plane on which he set his mother was in great contrast to the eroticism of his various day-to-day experiences. As long as these experiences didn't get too serious, it was fine, a game, a hunt, an escape." Thus the separation of eroticism—from Oedipal attraction.

From Ellington's perspective then, there are two kinds of women. Women who remain lasting partners and those who are a "passing fancy;" women who are, in essence, entertainment. They help separate the erotic from the permanent relationship.

Some psychoanalytic theorists believe that creative people have difficulties with intimacy. It is likely that creative people, particularly artists, are capable of intense intimate relationships perhaps enhancing their creative works. Eventually Ellington's life became more and more complicated because of the different sexual relationships and the problems he had keeping women away from him. His sister said it was "shocking" the way women were attracted to him. One of his favorite expressions, "We love you madly," became an overused comment— hollow and insincere and illustrative of the superficiality Ellington was capable of in these relationships. As the years passed, Ellington's self-control grew in all things except women. He had learned to control his appetite which was enormous and had become a problem, and he had dealt with his drinking. Ellington became religious and an avid student of the Bible.

Psychiatrists who had conversations with him alluded to his sadomasochistic tendencies. For example, he would be preparing for a concert of the utmost importance but would so hurt and incite people that they would want to hurt him back. They would downgrade him, tell him he was the lowest thing in the world, and end up by saying he wasn't even shit. This could be ten minutes before a performance was to begin, a time when he might especially have had a strong need for a particular performer. Ellington would "perversely do these things to provoke the man to walk off the show." This type of behavior is multi-determined and expresses issues of control as well as "tempting fate" and punishing himself as if to say "now if I'm successful I really deserve it." It may be a way of denying having been more successful and replacing his father in importance—which, of course, he did.

Mercer discusses his father's need to argue and win arguments "even if he had to adopt a stand he didn't believe in. This was part of his pleasure in manipulating people." It is as if Ellington found it necessary to drive people away when he felt an innate need for them either emotionally or for their professional services. There are examples of similar behavior with his own son. He would call Mercer in the middle of the night and start an argument, not because there was a cause or need for an argument, but because this would provide a reason for the call. Eventually, he would meet with Mercer and offer him something to eat or drink. The whole experience became an excuse for getting together. He could "save face without showing weakness, without showing he wanted somebody around him."

Ellington took a liberal attitude towards drugs and never admonished his band members for activities "society" might have viewed as wrong. He recognized that "artists were given to strange ways of living." He shaped the careers of many musicians, making stars of them, but avoided taking them from other band leaders. He also allowed freedom of choice in leaving his band for a better offer. The band of the Thirties stressed individualism, likely a substantial factor in Ellington's success. Ellington believed that a strongly disciplined band would not have the freedom to create and play. He remained clearly in charge, however chaotic the behavior may have seemed and he manipulated constantly. He once said, "No problem. I'm easy to please. I just want to have everybody in the palm of my hand." Thus, while Ellington's own behavior paralleled the "acceptable" white behavior of the day, he unabashedly tolerated the disorganization and irresponsible behavior on the part of his band men. The expectation was that of a more "natural" music and this contrast and perspective was an integral part of his character.

Primarily, Ellington wanted to do music and believed the people he had in his band were the ones to play it. When replacements entered the band, he would ask them to do what was natural and avoided giving directions for long periods of time. This characteristic led to a particular creative style and the arrangement and rearrangement of "links" in his music. He knew what he wanted pieces to sound like and, while controlling and subtly manipulating people, he allowed them the freedom to interject their own artistic creativity. He had less of a need to succeed than to be admired. On a practical level he shaped the career of many musicians and band leaders and had an uncanny sense of encouraging musicians to play above their natural ability. Vic Bellerby wrote, "Ellington's blues are conceived and developed from within the band. When playing his records, we realize that in no other orchestra can the individual soloist attain such dignity, for by some mysterious process, the individual solo becomes a contribution to a greater conception."

It was the essence of Ellington's character to break rules. He loved the out of the ordinary—one of the hallmarks of his genius. He discarded rules and involved himself in practices uncharacteristic of the creative talents of his day. With music, he created far more dissonance than was customary in bands of his time and left a fair amount of ambiguity and interpretive room. His music was not developed in accordance with the theories of music or art but rather created to produce a *response* in the listener. The principle of composition that became the cornerstone of his work was *contrast*. Variety, change, shocking effect, and the lack of adherence to the formal rules became Ellington trademarks.

Psychoanalyst Jerome Sashin described the concept of affect tolerance as it related to Duke Ellington. *Affect tolerance* is defined as "the ability to get in touch with one's feelings in their fullest intensity and hang on to them." In this regard, Ellington was able to develop the lyric quality of his music and make many innovations. This is the *sensuality* in Ellington's music—emotion is associated (attached) with the sound. Sashin pointed out that the hallmark of Ellington's genius was his ability to use harmonies and voicings that were, from a conventional perspective, not supposed to work. According to the textbooks, harmony and voicings were unorthodox and wrong. "This ability to take risks requires the capacity to tolerate enormous anxiety as one ventures into new and unknown territories." Sashin notes that throughout Ellington's life, when faced with stresses, disappointments and traumas, he could tolerate the affects that were evoked and use them to enhance his creativity. This *affect tolerance* is related to Ellington's capacity to fantasize, to verbalize affect, and to the intactness of what he calls the "inner container"—a derivative from the early parent-child relationship. This pertains to the internalization of the good aspects of the parents who were able to tolerate their own, as well as the child's, feeling states.

Ellington obviously felt loved and nurtured by his family and developed strong feelings of loyalty. The relationship with his "ideal" mother, however, seems to have produced its own set of problems in terms of his later inconstant intimate relationships. Nevertheless, he evidenced a strong ability to "hear and see in his mind combinations of sounds and colors that others simply could not." In addition to being able to fantasize auditory imagery, Ellington could also "fantasize visual imagery in remarkable ways." Sashin wrote that Ellington thought of music in terms of *color* and associated specific tones with specific emotions and each tone had a different color. These tones would become "colors in his mind's eye" and he would work with them, drawing upon his background as a painter for visual imagery in producing musical effects. And thus, he was able to tolerate enormous degrees of uncertainty, ambiguity and anxiety.

In this regard, *Black and Tan Fantasy* brought the band fame and bridged the gap of classical and Jazz music. It has been selected by music critics and intellectuals as being the single most important piece of Jazz in 1927. According to James Collier, "It was, to many of them, proof that Jazz was art, and this was true, not only in the United States but also in England, when the English intellectuals began to be excited by Jazz two or three years later."

In *Black and Tan Fantasy,* the touch of Chopin at the end is considered "a stroke of genius" and suggests musical sophistication. Collier wrote, "The importance of *Black and Tan Fantasy* to Jazz history should not be underestimated, for this, more than any other single record, suggested to critics that Jazz could be serious business. The melancholy aspects of this piece are a definitive reflection of decades of Black experience, trials and tribulations." In arranging this music Ellington removed himself from the obvious and worked with the unexpected.

Black and Tan Fantasy is another reflection of the strong visual sense of Ellington's music as well as a statement about life and the depth that music could represent it. The piece is likely a variation of New Orleans funeral marches or dirges which provide a spiritual background for the proceedings and, when the service ended at the grave, snap the crowd and bring them home in ragtime style. This music is a reflection of the reality-based experience of Blacks and their social oppression at any given time.

In *Black Beauty,* the 1928 song-portrait of Florence Mills, Ellington once again used contrasting phrases with the resultant effect of speech or dialogue approximating the African music of earlier times and also reflecting Ellington's increasing interest in the themes of Black culture. Three years later, he produced *Creole Rhapsody,* considered one of Ellington's finest and most completely integrated works. It involved unusual phrase lengths, is a genuinely extended composition and was a landmark in musical development. It was judged the best composition of the year in 1933 by the New York School of Music.

An interesting example of Black mythology cited by many authors is the association with trains. In the 19th and early 20th centuries, the train had almost a mythic meaning for American Blacks. It was the train that could take Blacks away from the cotton fields or the cold cities. Thousands of Blacks worked for the railroads in a variety of menial jobs but, most particularly, they held the prestigious job of Pullman porter. Black music of this period is full of references to railroads. Ellington used the effects of the train in many of his pieces, perhaps the most famous of which is *Daybreak Express,* an Ellington classic. We experience the re-creations of color and delicate feeling rather than protest. The piece audibly demonstrates the starting and stopping of a train with all its inherent romantic desire. Four of Ellington's finest impressionistic works are devoted to mechanical transportation—three of them deal with the steam train. The train was the cradle for the majority of his compositions and a place where he spent much of his life. He was proud of the rail cars and accommodations available to him, especially when traveling in the South. One Southerner was told, "This is how the President travels." Ellington described the refuge the train provided with its soothing metallic rhythm conducive to writing music. This was also a refuge from the segregation in the South.

Ellington was very superstitious and had many ritualistic concerns. This included wearing certain colors, a preference for certain numbers, not shaking hands while eating, refusing to give or receive gifts of shoes, a phobic reaction to drafts or being near open windows, a fear of being shipwrecked, and many others. He liked the number thirteen. He was a hypochondriac, was phobic about illnesses, and took lots of vitamins. He was extremely secretive—a profile behind the mask.

These neurotic traits are by-products of conflict resolution—an attempt to psychologically "work out" deeper conflicts. The psyche arrives at an accommodation we psychiatrists call "compromise formation." It is as if the psyche is saying, "You have not really resolved what you are afraid of and I will allow you to substitute this "little" symptom in its place." Dramatically, Mercer wrote, "I firmly believe that from around 1950 onward, Ellington began to develop a pronounced form of *paranoia*. He believed different things on different sets of people. In world events he believed prominent men were often influenced to act wrongly or immorally by women, who were in the background. He'd take headlines and check back to prove his theory."

Once again, the underlying hostility and distrust toward women manifests itself. On at least one occasion he surprised a group of people during a party by airing his belief in a "faggot Mafia." He went on to recount how homosexuals hired their own kind whenever they could and how, when they achieved executive status, maneuvered to keep "straight" guys out of influential positions.

Yet one of the most important attachments of Ellington's life was to Billy Strayhorn, an overt homosexual. An entire book is needed to describe the genius and musical contributions of "Strays." Strays joined the band as an arranger in 1940. The affectionate relationship with Ellington was reciprocated and some describe their relationship as being so close it was sexual but not in the physical sense. Strayhorn played a role in everything Ellington wrote from 1940 on and is especially known for *Take The A Train*. Ellington said their relationship could be described as a blending of their brain waves. Strayhorn's death was deeply traumatic for Ellington and he likely never recovered.

Paternal identification for Ellington was absent and with it the internal structure to deal with powerful psychological forces. Men learn control and develop identification in the relationship to a father figure. Destructive forces that arise in the course of development become directed and resolved. With Ellington, the destructive impulses manifested themselves from time-to-time in verbally sadistic behavior. He also wished for a daughter—a noncompetitive rival. He was triumphant over his father which is not healthy when there is no concomitant identification, and he used his son for his own glorification. As a result of the early psychological experiences—the closeness to his mother and relationship to a passive although loving father— Ellington had problems dealing with aggressive and hostile feelings and developed a *reaction formation* buttressed by numerous superstitions and rituals. The reaction formation involves denying hostility and replacing it with "kindness" or praise but never resolving the underlying anger. The ritualistic behaviors provide a method of warding off the "return of the repressed"—the early and later developmental influences that have been hidden in the psyche and threaten to break into consciousness. In Ellington's situation, he likely had repressed a fantasized "vengeful" father. When a young boy replaces the father in importance in the family, especially in connection with the mother, guilt develops along with the fantasy of retaliation by the father—the repressed vengeful father. None of this is on the surface. Some of these traits were later used constructively, especially the equation of color with musical sounds. Feelings are associated with colors and sound, which then displaces the anxiety from the original source. Feelings become a collective or creative alternative.

One example of reaction formation with Ellington occurred with his oversolicitous and complimentary behavior toward a nightclub owner with whom he was engaged in a dispute. Rather than stand his ground, Ellington complimented the man on his necktie and said he would agree to his demands if they could switch neckties. His autobiography is another example of avoiding negatives and complimenting everyone. It was the neurotic compromise formation that continued to manifest itself in lifelong hypochondriasis—his fear of being injured or sick.

Ellington did not like "categories" and one of his favorite compliments was that something was "beyond category" meaning that it could not be classified or equaled. Yet he looked for "flaws" in his sexual partners, something that was also "beyond category."

Duke Ellington was disdainful of academic degrees and formal institutions but he did display the honorary degrees bestowed on him. Formal training implied adhering to rules and, from Ellington's perspective, a lack of creativity. He did not like rules in anything and did not wanted to be involved with anything that anybody had already set down in a pattern. There was always an element of mischievousness in Ellington's personality and character—always an element of "stirring up the pot," and at times this was detrimental to the smooth functioning of the band. Sometimes he would struggle with problems that had already been solved by others simply because he did not want to ask others for help. He went looking for new ways to "solve" these problems. He was conscious of appearances and did not like the word "Jazz" because it related to sex, at least in the early days, and was a word used by the lowly elements of society in association with orgies.

Mercer mentions that the only time Ellington was "off guard" was when he was writing his music. Ellington would "spend many hours in despondent moods in motels, essentially expressing his feelings through his music…. His love of peace and tranquillity was expressed in his tone colors." The happy tunes were written during happy days and the sad pieces when he was sad or lonely. Ellington always wrote what he felt, never in contrast to his mood.

The unorthodox aspect of Ellington's style is understandable from the perspective of his stubbornness and predilection for breaking rules. He would argue a point for the sake of arguing. Discarding a rule was a source of inspiration which helped shape his work and the improvisation that went along with it. He played and wrote from something deep within—"soul."

The ambiguity of his work is characterized by other aspects of ambiguity in his life. I wish to emphasize that almost all of his best work was done with an image or a mood and not specifically with a musical or mathematical idea. He needed a psychological "prod" and without this would shift into a state of boredom and, although producing, the works would be somewhat monotonous. The mood had to be expressed for the best work and the visual image that reflects the mood and sentimental nostalgia permeates throughout Ellington's fanatical defense of privacy. This probably had negative effects on his lyrics which did not suit his music because the fit was poor. According to James Collier, "The problem lay in Duke's unwillingness to expose himself, his need always to fend off intimate inquiry, his inability to really unbutton himself, except for very few people on rare occasions…. Except for his sister Ruth, I don't know anybody who really gets close to Duke."

In writing lyrics, and certainly with the preparation and presentation of the three *Sacred Concerts*, the complex construction of form and content was unmatched. This separation, according to Collier, was "to avoid letting the world know what he was thinking and feeling." Even when he was dying, it was not acceptable to let others know that he was not the strong, competent person completely in control. Yet, in his music, he was able to go beyond the artistic impulse to the unconsidered feelings of the depth of his psyche, delivering these feelings to the safe haven of music and not words. Therein lies his genius. This, in a man who is manipulating circumstances involving musicians, gangsters, show business people, agents and the American racist culture as well. He had the capacity "to be concerned, but removed," yet to instill in his musical creations his own feeling state, all the while willing to endure disorder in doing so. In this respect, Duke Ellington acted on the feelings of himself and others in the true sense of producing art as an expansion of one's own psyche in communication with the psyche of its recipients.

I am reminded of Joseph Campbell's comment, "...*and where we had thought to travel outward we shall come to the center of our existence.*"

4

THE OBJECT AND THE DREAM: MARK ROTHKO

"What is paint after all? Colored dirt."
– Philip Guston

Psychoanalysis provides an avenue to explore unconscious determination in creativity. While it may fall short of explaining the inherent meaning of an artist's work, it does allow for a depth of understanding of the artist himself—where he is "coming from" as well as allowing for an "interpretation" that can be openly discussed. The genius of Mark Rothko cannot be understood—let alone appreciated—with psychoanalysis alone, but we do learn something of his motivation, his drive and perhaps his "intuitive sense." If Rothko were alive, he would likely deny any psychological interpretation of his work or himself. He did not think much of psychoanalysis, possibly because of its "reductionistic" perspective.

In attempting to understand Rothko, we must again consider the issue of unresolved grief and childhood loss. Tragedy and pain are apparent in much of his work which he characterized as "The Spirit of Myth—generic to all myths at all times." He professed a kinship with "primitive and archaic art" that also has a kinship to the Jungian unconscious. One may think of Rothko's philosophical aesthetic as the foundation of his oeuvre. Art critics and historians do not deal directly with the psychodynamic issues in his work—especially as a partial motivating factor to the art. The psychoanalytical studies of Martha Wolfenstein's on preadolescent and childhood parent loss are paramount in considering Rothko the man.

Mark Rothko lost his father when he was eleven years old. In accordance with psychoanalytic understanding, Rothko *internalized* (hypercathected the internal object) the image of his father, thus keeping him "alive" in his unconscious. This psychodynamic phenomenon leads to conflict as well as attachment because there is no escape or resolution of the "internalized relationship"—it is kept to (in) the self.

This early loss experience predisposes the individual to recurrent depressions and Rothko was alternately angry and depressed. His fantasies as an adult were hostile. Early loss may lead to symptoms such as eating disorders, attachment problems, and acute sensitivity to adult losses. Rothko engaged in bouts of overeating with resultant obesity and self-image problems. His physician, Albert Grokest, once said that Rothko's greatest sources of consolation were "alcohol and calories." His continual arguing with his first wife, Mell, contributed to her becoming an alcoholic as well.

Rothko attempted to assuage his father's loss (and keep him alive) by attending synagogue every day for a year although none of the other family members attended. He also continued identifying with his father's dissident politics and Marxist ideas. Rothko's quality of mistrust was solidified at this point. In his Yale yearbook for the class of 1925, where others list activities and interests, Rothko lists the date of his father's death.

Although Rothko's father died in 1914 at the age of 55, the result of colon cancer, this was the man's *second* abandonment of his son. The first occurred when the father departed for the United States, leaving the seven-year-old Rothko in the care of his mother. The final abandonment, at age 11, resulted in Rothko turning his back on the Jewish religion and religious order and produced an open rebellion. He was bitter about the father loss and swore he would never go to synagogue again. It is easier to be angry than sad. A primitive source of anger associated with loss, or impending loss, may have its roots in phylogentic development.

Another manifestation of Rothko's loss was the mistrust he showed later in life, especially his mistrust of male authority figures. For example, his physician mentioned that on the first visit, Rothko did not allow him to do a physical examination! Authority figures can become a target for anger, and, on the other hand, can become an object of dependency in the search for a father substitute. This behavior may also manifest as passivity in close male relationships. In Rothko's case, art became an avenue to freedom. However, Mark Rothko produced tragic art.

Alternate behaviors of isolation and attachment are noted throughout Rothko's life. His feelings of isolation, compounded by depression, led to his suicide in 1970. Rothko said, "The only serious thing is death, nothing else is to be taken seriously." His work represents a preoccupation with death and intimations of mortality. Especially in the work of the 1950s and 1960s, one finds an absence of people, places and objects. The art contains a sense of solitude, emptiness, diffusion and loss.

Rothko insisted, "My art lives and breathes." Thus, something had to "live." He kept his *transitional object* alive as a form of *undoing* of the loss he experienced. His art lived and thus, his father lived. Nevertheless, he maintained an "abiding core of anger" according to John Fischer. Rothko has been described as being a "combative" person with an "adversarial view of human nature." This may have contributed to his being an "outsider," further reinforcing his bitterness and depression. The image emerges of a hefty, bearlike, man with a voracious appetite and an alcohol problem. He smoked, became portly, developed gout.

Later, when his mother died in 1949, Rothko became overtly depressed. His psychological makeup was further reinforced in the direction of cynicism and bitterness—multi-determined by a host of events and losses. There are creative similarities in his behavior with that of Duke Ellington (chapter 3) when "Duke" lost his mother, although Ellington had a happier and more substantially nurturing childhood and could sustain later losses better.

Rothko's mother, Kate, was energetic, forceful and practical. He perceived her to be very powerful although lacking in affection. She never understood his art but always supported, protected and defended him. Rothko often complained that the "world" never really understood his art, yet he never complained about his mother's lack of comprehension. Kate was a woman who always wanted to be included in *everything* even in her later years. Family anecdotes by her grandchildren attest to the driving force of her energy when they describe her as "bustling." In ways of the world she could be very passionate and strong-willed—a determined woman described as a "tough cookie," "very strong," "a very powerful woman, center stage in every group." Many considered her to be the "driving force" behind the family. In many respects, Rothko was closer to the women of the family, meaning his sister and mother, especially after the death of his father.

Kate Rothkowitz was the woman "behind" Rothko. Eventually he painted *Portrait of Rothko's Mother* which depicts a woman both lonely and bitter, oppressed and oppressive. This demonstrates her attitude of tough resentment, not surprising in light of her experiences in Czarist anti-Semitic Russia, the struggles in America, and the loss of her husband. Rothko's mother was no dreamer and her lack of warmth, combined with her determination and sorrow are all evident in his portrait. There was little else for him to connect with.

Eventually Rothko separated himself from his mother, at least geographically, by his move to New York City. The demonstration of closeness and distance is depicted in his artistic work, especially the 1936 piece *The Rothko Family*, which evidences the "tensions and separations" of family experience, the intensity of the father-son relationship, and, once again, the brooding mother. In both portraits one notes more "melancholy than warmth" in his mother, a likely depiction of his innate understanding of her and his partial identification with her. It is how she *feels*. Rothko could identify with her, understand her desperation and yet need to separate from her. Thus, his artistic productions— silent works of empathy, yet distance and separation.

Mark Rothko was a Russian Jew born in Dvinsk in 1903. His city had about 90,000 people—at least half of which were Jewish and therefore exposed to the harsh political realities of Czarist Russia. Dvinsk was an industrial town, a busy railroad junction and, understandably, a haven for radical political groups. Rothko's father, Jacob, was a pharmacist with a reasonable income who provided a strong religious education for his son. He was also a political radical and the person his son later used as his model for political ideas. Mark Rothko spoke of his father with reverence as a "man of great character, great intellect," a teacher and a moral counselor. The father had come from a generation of Russian intellectuals and was "an icon" for his youngest child.

Most likely, Rothko memorized the *Talmud* and learned Hebrew scriptures. The poems in his notebook were written in Hebrew and clearly he maintained a "tribal loyalty" throughout his life. An early memory was of his family talking about the massacre of Jews by Cossacks. Some art historians speculate as to whether Rothko sustained the rectangular image of a mass grave, thereby producing his later preoccupation with the rectangle of his paintings from the 1950s and 1960s. We will never know. Certainly he kept in mind and celebrated Jewish survival.

Rothko had three older siblings. His father emigrated to America to follow a brother. Three years later he brought his wife, son and daughter to Portland, Oregon. The initial abandonment by his father was followed by an even more severe abandonment when his father died within months of the family's arrival in Portland. Rothko never felt at home in the United States and never forgave this move.

Although Rothko's memories of Russia involved persecutory violence, he had lost his culture, language, friends and home. In some respects, he resisted assimilation, never really "belonging." He remained a stranger in a strange land. Migration can create an identity crisis when the self loses its anchor. Critics remark that Rothko's *Street Scene* represents a suspension between two worlds and, sadly distrustful, belongs to neither one. Likely, he was inwardly detached in Portland because his mother had to care for her sick husband for those few months before he died. The family was also left in severe financial straits and Rothko became the "poor relation." He worked hard at everything he did and was given work by his relatives whom he resented because they were "rich." He felt patronized and this has been described as the "Jewish philistinism that Rothko loved to hate."

Brother Moise describes Rothko as a "high-strung" and naturally sensitive child. He suffered a calcium deficiency and likely ate the plaster on the walls in an attempt to replace the element. Moise said Rothko was "a very, very sick child." He developed a ravenous appetite (in later years friends remarked how they liked to watch him eat) and became a hypochondriac. As an adult, he was constantly fretting over his body.

Working to absorb a new culture, Rothko was strongly influenced by the Oregon landscape of the West Hills, with its mountains in the distance, sense of vastness and, at least then, emptiness. As a paper boy, Rothko had to compete with others in the new Capitalistic world and, as a chubby kid, often lost sales when in competition with others. He was intensely committed to education and went from the first grade in 1913—not speaking any English, to the third grade in 1914, advancing to fifth grade by Spring term. He completed the last four years of primary school in three. In 1921, eight years after his arrival in Portland, Rothko graduated from Lincoln High. He found the high school program "ridiculously easy."

As an adolescent, Mark Rothko showed remarkable skill in debating and was considered "smart," "contentious," and a person who "talked a lot," characteristics that remained throughout his life. This chubby boy had strong interests in literature and social studies, was highly opinionated and quite outspoken, especially on liberal politics—something that wasn't accepted readily. His family "applauded the

Russian revolution" and Rothko said he "grew up as an anarchist." He admired Emma Goldman because she opposed authority so strongly. During the Palmer raids in 1918, Goldman was deported to Russia. An avid reader, Rothko developed a strong interest in music, which remained extremely important throughout his life. He did like to draw, and, like Andrew Wyeth (chapter 2), considered himself self-taught as an artist. Interestingly, he took no art classes in high school or at Yale. He did not depend on, nor trust, male authority. His later works reflect a humanistic content.

Rothko's vision was that life was irrational. In high school he was a target of anti-Semitic slurs and was excluded, along with other Jews, from the debating society at Lincoln High. As a result, he started his own debating group. His outsider status was reinforced and his writing during this period reflected "a depressed sense of grim necessity…an endless and hollow task." His emptiness and despair was clearly in evidence at age 17. Vulnerability to depressions and narcissistic "hurts" remained throughout his life. James Breslin wrote that by 1949 these feelings were "transformed into empty bands of colored light." With all of the exclusion and turmoil at Lincoln, and continuing to be the butt of sneering jokes, Rothko intellectualized his anger by channeling it into political debate. He was a foreigner at a touchy, sensitive time in American history. Naturally his loyalty would be suspect and his position insecure. He was pressured to conform politically and patriotically.

Rothko also wrote poetry and his *Salutation* alludes to a search for happiness in *this* world. *Radical Awareness* addresses the danger and embarrassment of cultural differences as well as racial and familial attachments. *Walls of Mind* deals with issues of the past. Significantly, Rothko wrote, *"I became a painter because I wanted to raise painting to the level of poignancy of music and poetry."*

Rothko won a scholarship to Yale University and enrolled with the intention of entering a profession. Yale, in Rothko's day, was a school where no Jew had ever been appointed to the permanent faculty. At Yale, Rothko discovered institutionalized anti-Semitism. In 1921 the quota system was described as necessary to repulse the "Jewish invasion." He was described as a "Falstaffian character, amiable, delightful" amidst an environment that considered Jews to be "pushy...grinds." He lived off-campus, again the "poor relation" separated from campus life.

He sought out the company of other Russian Jews who shared his interest in art, music and literature. At the end of his first semester, his tuition scholarships were converted to loans, and once again Rothko was betrayed by authority. He was forced to work as when his father died. Rothko liked to tell the story about how he deliberately would spill food on students when he worked in the dining hall in order to give business to the cleaners!

At Yale, Rothko was recalled as being "brilliant" and "well read." He helped develop the Yale *Saturday Evening Pest* which was skeptical of the university education system and used terms such as "soul-less," "lifeless," and "empty." In an article he wrote titled, "The House of The Dead," he discussed his experiences in Portland and at Yale. Although he had moved from his rented room in the Jewish ghetto to the dormitory in his second year, by the Spring of 1923 he became disillusioned about an educational career and quit Yale. This was another complete break and a turning point in his life. Simon Whitney wrote that Rothko was "completely scornful of the Yale establishment and the students. I suppose this is one reason he left." Rothko was breaking the traditional Jewish emphasis to be a professional and to maintain economic security.

After Yale, Rothko left for New York, survived at odd jobs and remained a voracious reader. He said, "I happened to wander into an art class to meet a friend who was taking the course. All the students were sketching this nude model—and right away I decided that was the life for me." He enrolled in the Art Students League, visited Portland for a brief time, then returned to New York and studied under the artistic influence of Max Weber, who, according to art and music historian Rudi Blesh, was a *truly modern* artist.

Max Weber is considered one of the more interesting of the eclectic vanguard modernists who merged Analytical Cubism, African primitivism and Matisse's synthetic Expressionism. He strongly influenced Rothko over a two-year period. Dore Ashton writes that Weber's stress on expression was a guiding principle for Rothko as he learned from other painters, and emphasized self-teaching. Weber taught, "A form must be more than a form—it must suggest the *sacred*. A color must be more than a color" (emphasis added).

Rothko had clearly learned the "direct expression of feelings." (His *Serene* paintings of 1950 suggest a primitive darkness—a way out of the cave.) For years Rothko painted realistically—a blend of Expressionism and Surrealism, including still lifes and landscapes avoiding perspective with a shallow picture plane. He was very innovative, experimenting with a variety of mediums. Of drawing and painting nudes he wrote, "I thought it was marvelous. I was intoxicated by it."

Shortly before this, while visiting Portland, he had substantial exposure to the theater which may have continued his interest in describing his paintings as "dramas" and his shapes as "performers." He had become theatrical—dramatic—and it's interesting to find his sense of life projected in the paintings—the transitional object that comes to life. The art that lives and breathes.

4. THE OBJECT AND THE DREAM—MARK ROTHKO

Although the separation from his family was difficult and slow, once removed from "dull and provincial" Portland (which he seemed to dislike immensely), he was free to develop in New York. He said he would have become a "bum" if he remained in Portland. He was out of "the House of the Dead" and emotionally and sensuously intoxicated by his newfound direction, his "noble ideal."

As with the artist Helen Hardin, (chapter 6), Rothko defied traditional taboos; in his case, the traditional Jewish taboo against iconic images. He was stubborn and had to go his own way. As Breslin notes, "Rothko entered a profession with a Gentile tradition, no training and no supportive tradition of his own. He broke "with the ties of family, class, religion, ethnicity, etc." In this respect we may compare Rothko's courage with Duke Ellington who did something very similar but without separating from his ethnicity or religion. Ellington had to be innovative in a way that defied familial tradition and white society. Rothko substituted art for politics and now had a direction—a "sacred calling." Stanley Kunitz called Rothko "The last Rabbi of Western art." Rothko faced the ordeal of poverty, self-sacrifice, and of being alone, hungry, and monastic. The idea of being self-punishing had its appeal, however, because his sense of guilt about father—and perhaps success itself—could be assuaged by deprivation. He was free to explore "transcendental experience." In his work at least, Rothko could be sensual, seductive and "religious." He was freed from convention and political-geographic ties. Rothko, as a lonely man, chose a profession that fostered further loneliness and isolation. His expressionist scenes of the late 1920s reflect urban isolation and solitary life.

In 1928 Rothko met Lewis Browne, a Rabbi turned author who hired him to illustrate *The Graphic Bible*. This relationship turned out to be a major disappointment for Rothko, leaving him feeling betrayed and in great financial debt. He was publicly humiliated by a lawsuit that received coverage in the *New York Times* and he even had to pay court costs. Once again he was let down by authority—paternal, academic, and now judicial. However, the battle between Rothko and Browne was more than a legal one—it was Rothko against the system and all aspects of authority, especially Jewish authority and to some extent artistic authority. This experience confirmed Rothko's suspicion of affluent authority and one observer noted, "Just a few years after leaving New Haven, Rothko had replaced its genteel WASP anti-Semitism with Browne's genteel Jewish anti-Semitism." In the law suit with Browne, Rothko was both self-assertive and self-destructive in dramatizing his conflict with authority. Later he was also betrayed by his accountant Bernard Reis. "Rothko, it seems, has some propensity for putting himself in the way of wolves, the better to assure himself that he was a lamb. Wolves are not hard to find." Once again, and repeatedly, we find evidence of self-destructive behavior.

In 1929 Rothko found a job at the Center Academy in Brooklyn—a school for children. He had substantial interest in children and in the development of artistic creativity in children, primarily as it related to the entire experience in life—the *Weltenschaung.* He differentiated between sheer skill and a skill that is linked to the spirit. "Between the painter who paints well and the artist whose works breathe life and imagination" one finds the essence of creativity.

Rothko taught at the Academy for more than twenty years and immersed himself in the creative process of children. His interests in art education were immense, especially as related to self-expression *in conjunction with* a total artistic statement—not just one of personal expression. He sought something much greater than personal ex-pression: "We favor the simple expression of the complex thought...

there is no such thing as a good painting about nothing…the subject is crucial and only that subject-matter is valid which is tragic and timeless."

In his late twenties, Rothko was influenced by Milton Avery who painted using color then adding allusions and distortions to his work. The work, however, went beyond the personal. Avery was s kind of "anchor" for Rothko. His friendship and family life added to their relationship in a very empathic-human way. This was a natural and normal personification of a "calling" that continuously inspired Rothko who responded to the warmth and tenderness of Avery's figures with "clarification of purpose." The relationship was especially important because Rothko distrusted and questioned the world of men. Contemporaneously, Rothko also developed a relationship with Adolph Gottlieb who explored the art world of pictographs, symbols and signs that projected images of archaic prehistoric paintings he termed "disinterred relics." Gottlieb and Rothko met frequently and talked a great deal.

Rothko was a large, physically hulking man who produced room-sized canvases. Rudi Blesh noted "He himself is variable. Outgoing. He fills a room or the street where he stops you to talk. Indrawn and brooding, he shrinks like the echo of a cry. But whatever may be said of his excesses, Mark Rothko is never piddling."

In 1932 Mark Rothko met Edith Sacher from Brooklyn. She was 20 years old when they married on November 12; Rothko was 29. Although physical opposites (Rothko was tall, burly with a wide nose and thick lips; Edith was five feet, four-and-a-half inches, slender and graceful). They shared artistic aspirations and interests and married three days after Franklin Roosevelt was elected President. Between 1936 and 1939, Rothko worked for the WPA—Works Projects Administration—which was "a godsend to artists." His marriage helped anchor him further although he appears to have been more of a dependent than an equal in the relationship. His wife, in writing, referred to him as a "very sweet boy" (Rothko was 33 at the time) and she seems to have had to take care of him. Rothko viewed Edith as being "materialistic" although he had his own problems dealing with the material benefits of success. They separated in 1937, reconciled but continued to have violent arguments. He referred to his wife as being "bourgeois." Edith was described as being "chilly" and a "cold fish." She is said to have had an "inflated view of herself and of her work as an artist" and likely was bluntly insulting to some of Rothko's artist friends. Others have described her as "a modern woman before her time" and as being "very opinionated," "a strong person," manipulative— some of the same descriptions used to portray Rothko's mother.

Rothko was sloppy, vulnerable to self-injury and careless. The word "slob" has been used to depict his behavior at home. James Breslin wrote that Edith behaved as a mother to make him presentable so she would "not be ashamed of him." Rothko was also very moody and tended to dominate Edith who lived in his shadow. Edith had become financially successful and aggressively pursued her own business interests, turning away from her husband. Whether adultery on Rothko's part was an issue is debatable. She apparently felt she was being used with little emotional return and their divorce was final by 1945.

In 1938 Rothko became a citizen of the United States and in 1940 began to use the name Rothko; discarding the "witz" in his name— thus removing the "son of" in external reality while maintaining the internal consistency (object consistency) of his "lost object"—his father. His loyalty to family tradition and his cultural background found expression in his strong feelings about the Jewish Holocaust. When offered an opportunity to display his works in Germany he refused! The sense of the tragic, mystery, and dread permeated his work and his life.

According to Breslin, Rothko confided to Robert Motherwell that as an infant he had been bound tightly in swaddling clothes, not an unusual child-rearing practice in Russia. Perhaps this related to a sense of "smothering" in relationships and the boundary problems he had throughout his life with intimate relationships. He is also said to have made the statement, "Jews have hurt me most." The rupture of the marriage was painful for him and during this period he is described as having had a "serious breakdown."

Rothko has been described by John Fischer as a man "whose gentleness is only a little less terrifying than his anger." He once told Fischer, former editor-in-chief of *Harpers,* about his commission to paint a series of large canvases for the walls of the most exclusive room in The Four Seasons, a very expensive restaurant in New York's Seagram Building. Rothko described the situation as "a place where the richest bastards in New York will come to feed and show off...I accepted this assignment as a challenge, with strictly malicious intentions. I hope to paint something that will ruin the appetite of every son-of-a-bitch who ever eats in that room. If the restaurant would refuse to put up my murals, that would be the ultimate compliment. But they won't. People can stand anything these days." Rothko wanted to use a dark, somber palette and make the viewers feel like they were *trapped* in a room where all the doors and windows were bricked up "so that all they can do is butt their heads forever against the wall...I keep my *malice* constantly in mind. It is a very strong motivating force." The murals were never hung in the dining room he so despised.

This verbal expression of his rage has its origins in early developmental experiences and eventual parent loss. He stressed malice behind this Seagram project "painting for or against the rich." This presents problems. He was "combative," but as an insider felt "contaminated." Even *success* was a problem. It was conflictual. Van Gogh could not accept his success and Rothko had significant problems accepting recognition and wealth. His anxiety about the purchase of a house was such that he had to attribute this action to the "pressure" of his wife and accountant. Wealth represented a state of no longer being poor and he had to say he was pressured into it. He bemoaned the separation from his artist friends, both geographically and economically. As James Breslin, wrote in his biography of Mark Rothko, "If he was not poor, marginal or wronged, who was he?" His identification was so intensely negative that conflicts developed and his abuse of alcohol likely served to assuage his conscience and guilt over success as well as the internal losses he experienced. This restless, lonely, yet gregarious man is described by Anne-Marie Levine: "He'd been fighting the world for so long he felt severely compromised by situations when the world would pay him homage."

Simultaneously, Rothko seriously feared the younger artists whom he thought would replace him. He wanted success—and to keep it, yet had mixed feelings about wealth and poverty. He created art works to provide a place for himself and to achieve the success he desired. Yet he isolated himself, was vulnerable and suspicious and prone to despair. What a burden! However, through all of this his wish for creativity was sustained.

Rothko married Mary Alice Beistel (Mell) in 1945, the same year his divorce from Edith was finalized. Mell was a warm, affectionate woman with strong interests in writing and theatre. Although Rothko said that marriage was incompatible with an artist's life, he readily married her and she sustained him.

As with Duke Ellington, when Rothko's mother died he portrayed his grief in art. Scott Joplin did the same thing with the death of his daughter, Monisha. One of the outstanding characteristics of artists is their ability to take "feeling" from tragedy and create from it. Rothko's paintings, just after the loss of his mother, are filled with charged feeling and served as a release for his despair—they provided a transcendence. Some have described this release as a "nurturing beauty." The psychological hurt thus advanced Rothko's work.

By 1950, Rothko was painting in his classic style stacking up rectangles of glowing color. In the spring, he sailed to Europe visiting England, France and Italy. In 1951 he was appointed Assistant Professor, Department of Design, Brooklyn College and held that position until his termination in June 1954. "If we awaited for sympathetic environments, our visions which are new would never have to be invented and our convictions never spoken... My idea of a school is Plato's Academy, where a man learns by conversing with *men of conse-quence*" (emphasis added).

Rothko's painting style is described as never being gentle, "a muscular and fervent expressionist until 1939... The large canvases in the 1940s and...then all at once...light hit Rothko...*the light of time and space, unconcerned even with man's existence*...it was light and silence seen and heard as one and the same thing." Further noted by George Heard Hamilton, former Director of the Yale University Art Gallery, "In Rothko's measured space, movement and silence turn into themselves. The format of rectangular shapes adds ambiguity in space." Blesh said Rothko's canvases, with their simplicity and size, bring you into the picture. This, of course, was Rothko's intent.

With strong needs to separate from his mother, he also identified with her. It is said that she even referred to Rothko as "my son, the painter." After her death in 1949 he experienced deprivation. Following her loss, he created works that were large, beautiful, aggressive and sensuous. The paintings were, at the same time, invasive and distanced. Bonnie Clearwater noted, "It is possible to be violently against them—it is impossible not to be involved." One artist said that "one could warm your hands in front of his paintings." Rothko's vision was one of a "higher experience meant for meditation—he rose above the mundane and attempted an external statement—mythic."

Rothko is described by Milton Avery as being "very verbal and told fabulous stories, a continual raconteur" and by Blesh as someone who "boiled and fumed" and sulked. Blesh wrote, "But a different Rothko is to be found in his paintings, wherein all the torments, great and little but abiding, have been fused together into one bright, silent frame... Only Rothko, being *finally himself,* is not amazed" (emphasis added).

John Fischer also made note of Rothko's penchant for talk. "Talk, as I later found out, was a necessity of life for him, like breathing." Talking, eating, drinking—obsessive orality. He also craved music and was influenced greatly by it. The abstractness of music appealed to Rothko's desire to immerse himself in meaning with pre-logical experience. Even his paintings bypass the world of objects with their illusive "simplicity."

He initially developed this perspective with spaces extending to infinity and the floating-fluid nature of watercolors in association with the myth-like elements of other painters such as Miro. Thus his work represented a natural language—ephemeral and intuitive, reflecting his own states of mind. This private sense of enchantment was to become "public,"—a search for a basic language to communicate basic truths. One is reminded of the ancient cave drawings of Lascaux with their timelessness and universal statement.

Art critic Robert Hughes describes Mark Rothko as having an early childhood that "...was scarred by memories of mob violence against Jews. Rothko grew into a touchy, academically-gifted scholar-ship boy, fiercely attached to radical causes. Right up to 1970, the last year of his life, he maintain that he was an anarchist." Rothko, in turn, had an interesting view of critics, "I hate and distrust all art historians, experts and critics. They are a bunch of *parasites*, feeding on the body of art. Their work not only is useless, it is misleading. They can say nothing worth listening to about art or the artist, aside from personal gossip." Part of Rothko's opinion is based on his belief that, "A painting doesn't need anybody to explain what it is about. If it is any good it speaks for itself, and a critic who tries to add to that statement is presumptuous."

Rothko's hatred was extensive. He detested "the whole machinery for the popularization of art—universities, advertising, museums and Fifty-seventh Street salesman." He refused to lend his pictures to group exhibits. "I believe that a painting can only communicate directly to the rare individual who happens to be in tune with it and the artist." He saw museums exhibiting his work as needing him—"They need me. I don't need them. This show will lend dignity to the Museum. It does not lend dignity to me." Contradictorily as an anarchist, he disapproved of the wealthy and questioned their taste. But they are the ones who could afford his paintings! He remained true to his interest in basic truths and inner character, and by the 1940's had arrived at his basic form—stratified blocks of color arranged on canvas.

Robert Hughes believes, "That Rothko had a religious vision of some kind is not in doubt. There was a deeply rabbinical streak in his character...and he hoped to express the sense of awe and numinous presence which had once been associated with the depiction of gods in art—but to do it *without the human figure*." Hughes speaks of Rothko using indeterminate space and refined sensuous color to depict the despair and elevation of the Old Testament. Hughes does not believe Rothko was successful in producing a religious statement as beautiful, deep and sensitive as his paintings were in allowing a "letting-go in the viewer. Rothko's work could not, in the end, support the weight of meaning he wanted it to have."

Rothko's first wife Edith thought his paintings conveyed a sense of magic bordering on the religious, but Rothko denied it. He was responding, perhaps, to his own pain, "Not a mystic. A prophet perhaps...I just paint the woes already here." Others saw his work as mystical, transcendental and religious, i.e., "celebrating the death of a civilization." Interestingly, regarding the Seagram mural work, he decided to have the paintings placed in a nondenominational chapel in Houston. He describes the Houston Chapel work as an example of this failure.

John Fischer also writes that on two occasions Rothko said his work might represent some deeply hidden religious impulse. In fact, during a visit to Pompeii, Rothko is reported to have said he felt a "deep affinity" between his own work and the House of Mysteries there, especially relating to the expanses of somber color. He made another interesting comment during a visit to an ancient Greek colony. "I have been painting Greek temples all my life without knowing it."

The religious connection of art and ancient life has been in the teaching through pictorial representation in the churches of Europe. These works were intimately related to the religious needs of the people and the teachings of the Church. Fischer notes that art, through time, has become more esoteric as the religious teaching and functions have been taken over by other modalities, and attributes some of Rothko's disillusionment to the more materialistic functions of art and the commercial expectations. This is one aspect of a creative individual's losses but the bitterness he expressed through life, the "orality," the hostility and conflicted meanings and relationships in his experience, speak to a much deeper "hurt"—something we may term "narcissistic injury."

Fischer notes the lack of deep meaning secondary to the utilitarian aspect of art as a contributing cause of Rothko's anger, especially as it relates to the artist's message. He wanted to be evaluated for the meaning of his life's work.

Markedly relevant in regard to Rothko's psychological state are the comments of Robert Goldwater who described the last two years of the artist's work as making a break with the past—although continuing the vision. These paintings followed the sudden illness Rothko experienced—another deep narcissistic wound—with months of brooding. He was now at the edge of the abyss. Goldwater also notes that Rothko needed a "break" from the specifically religious purpose of the Chapel paintings before he could begin afresh, "Within the rhythm of Rothko's life, then, the period of these last works was a separate entity. It is, above all, the mood of the works themselves, and especially those done during the last year, that sets these final paintings apart...the somber spirit that pervades these last pictures." Rothko also knew these paintings were like nothing he had ever done. There was a brooding character to his work at this point—he lived in his tragic interior realm. Goldwater writes that the sense of these works was tragic—somber and sad. "By their presence they conveyed absence...the projection of despair."

In the later paintings, withdrawal contrasted with his previous works of coming forward. Goldwater wrote that Rothko was well aware of the reversal—the flat tones and suggestion of deep space—the visual and psychological, perhaps spiritual, distancing. He notes that these last pictures suggest loneliness and withdraw into themselves, rejecting the participation of the viewer. Most significantly he writes with the insight of a psychoanalyst, *"The sense of the tragic, then had been present in Rothko's work and as his art developed it dominated more and more of his paintings. He spoke of his desire for an art that would express the human condition—and so would perforce be a tragic art."* This is an explanation of the essence of Rothko's work. The colors darkened with time, black played a more prominent and "positive" decisive role in the work, the range of harmonies closer and the result more direct expression of mood. Goldwater has also captured aspects of Rothko's chronic depression, his sense of the tragic and of impending disaster. Death is ever-present. He spoke of "a clear preoccupation with death—all art deals with intimations of mortality."

Rothko's responses to the human situation were also, no doubt, influenced by his early religious training and his sense of mysticism— an attempt to sense the unknown, the spiritual—the deeply mysterious presence of God. Dore Ashton writes, "He was like a mystic in that he had an overwhelming private hunger for illumination, for personal enlightenment, for some direct experience—or at least the quality of that experience—*with the transcendent.* He was a mystic in the way Nietzsche described 'a mystic soul'...almost undecided whether it should communicate or conceal itself (emphasis added)."

Thus, the ambivalence. Rothko was convinced no one had ever fully understood his work. As Ashton writes, his canvases both reveal and conceal—they offer and they hold back. This is, of course, part of the appeal. This equivocation along with the use of light provides the mystery—the "longing for the universal experience of unity." Even Rothko's refusal of mysticism is an offering and withdrawal—his desire for the universal, the tragic and the transcendent is always there. The light then is a "light of revelation" which gradually extinguished itself. It was even partially concealed during his life—light illuminates and hides. The light is a light of spirituality—Rothko's ultimate goal! This spirituality was intimately connected to his sense of the tragic and summed up by his statement of art, "...a clear preoccupation with death—all art deals with intimations of mortality."

Near the end of his life, in 1968 or 1969, Rothko produced on paper some of the richest color works of his life. The paperworks have been described by Bonnie Clearwater in her book, *Mark Rothko Works on Paper,* as "works of daring iridescence... They generate a strong, constant glow." The surface of one of his last paintings is saturated with red acrylic paint—likely related to the colorful late paper works. I wonder if this is also related to Rothko's preoccupation and identification with Matisse's *The Red Studio*. In 1949, Rothko spent hours and hours before Matisse's painting. Near the end of his life he may have been creating or recreating his own version of this work—reflecting a fusion and strong attachment to Matisse psychologically. He was attuned to *The Red Studio* perhaps in a way that was unique to any other work.

In the spring of 1968 Rothko suffered an aneurysm of the aorta and was hospitalized for three weeks. As with many people who achieve "celebrity" status, their medical care becomes complicated by the intrusion of "actors" of consequence including agents, publicity people, and hangers on. This was so in Rothko's case with his accountant Reis superseding Rothko's physician Dr. Grokest. This pattern was to continue through Rothko's terminal depression. One observer noted, "He really died after he had that seizure." The dissecting aneurysm left him unable to paint for weeks. He became "resentful" and fearful.

As a physician, I have had personal and public experience with this frightening condition. Clearly Rothko developed a global depression around this time. His marital problems became worse and worse, as he had been fighting with Mell and they both had been drinking too much. Rothko's hypochondrical, demanding behavior intensified. Apparently he trusted and relied on Reis for financial and other support because, "I hate attorneys." He could not separate a global dislike from professional need.

In 1969, Rothko separated from his wife and children and moved into his studio. "Mine is a bitter old age." With the direction of Reis, he came under the care of Dr. Nathan Kline whose psychiatric emphasis was pharmacological, although he attempted to seek advice from his psychiatrist friend, Dr. Ruddick who, because he was a friend, could not treat Rothko. Drs. Ruddick and Grokest both felt Rothko was overmedicated on Sinequan and was "living on the brink." Rothko did not face up to the loss of self-esteem or the psychic pain he was experiencing. It was easier for him to try to solve his problem with pills, including sleeping pills and alcohol. We psychiatrists call this significant drop in self-esteem a "narcissistic hurt." There was no anticipation of happiness and he had still not mourned the loss of his mother. The treatment proceeded against Grokest's advice and to the medication regimen was added Valium.

Avoiding scrutiny of his psyche and being promised a quick cure, Rothko avoided introspection and used the pills and Scotch in an attempt to solve his problems. Quick to anger, wary of betrayal and dependent, he relied on Reis and Kline. Rothko's medicine cabinet was filled with medicines for anxiety, depression, sleeping problems, hypertension and gout.

In 1969 he also developed a relationship with Rita Reinhardt, a 40-year-old woman who pressed him to get a divorce from his wife. Rothko was 65 then and this new relationship further complicated and confused his outlook. No psychiatrist was working with him on these relationships. James Breslin writes that Rothko attempted to create "a romanticized version of his student days."

Mark Rothko's suicide on February 25, 1970 was ritualistic. He took substantial amounts of drugs, selected a double-edged blade which he held with Kleenex, removed his trousers and stood over a sink with the water on as he cut deeply into the arteries of his arms. He was found face up in a pool of blood. The autopsy report noted advanced heart disease and significant emphysema. Also mentioned are the lacerations in the *antecubital fossae* (the forearm where it folds), drug overdose, acute gastritis and acute barbiturate poisoning. His suicide was unequivocal, methodical and deliberate. Dr. Grokest wrote that it was "the deed of a man who had spent hours contemplating the violence he saw in his own paintings." He was found in the attitude of a Christ— as Breslin writes, the attitude of a demanding father and a submissive son.

5

MASK AND STEEL—
WHEN LIFE
IMITATES ART:
YUKIO MISHIMA

*"His was a battlefield without glory, a battlefield where none
could display deeds of valor: It was the front line of the
spirit.... What he was about to perform was an act in his
public capacity as a soldier, something he had never
previously shown his wife. It called for a resolution equal to the
courage to enter battle; it was a death of no less degree and
quality than death in the front line. It was his conduct on the
battlefield that he was now to display."*
Mishima
"Patriotism"

Kimitake Hiraoka, better known by his pen name Yukio Mishima, was born January 14, 1925 and died in spectacular fashion on November 25, 1970. He was 45 years old.

Mishima produced forty novels, eighteen plays, twenty volumes of short stories and essays and was nominated three times for the Nobel Prize. He acted in the firm version of his story, *Patriotism*, plunging a prop sword into his belly in what was to be a rehearsal for his actual suicide years later. His life was a quest for the merging of art and life—writing and action. His life *and* his death became high theater. His death was personal, cultural, religious and more. He believed that beauty, like life, is fleeting. He was a patriot and fervent nationalist who mastered the martial arts of karate and swordsmanship. He maintained a regimen of three intensive weight lifting workouts a week from 1955 on—a quest he described as "the ultimate verification of existence." This quest was necessary by the "language of the flesh"— "antithetical to words." He experienced trouble feeling alive and sought proof of his being. He acted these parts in daily life as well as on stage and screen in his own plays.

Mishima founded his own army, opposed the infiltration of western culture in Japan and maintained an erotic fascination with death— culminating in his own ritual suicide at a time *when he was unrivaled as the outstanding Japanese writer of his generation.*

His first book, *Forest In Full Bloom* written at age 16, was inspired by the poetic Japan of old—consistent with his scholarly knowledge of classical Japan—an aesthete in traditional culture as well as beauty. At the time of its publication, he chose his pseudonym, "Yukio Mishima." Mishima is the name of a village at the foot of Mt. Fuji; the name Yukio is said to make one think of snow.

Perhaps the "coldness" of this name is reminiscent of maternal loss. He was taken from his mother and reared by a sickly grandmother on his fiftieth day of life. He lived jealously coveted by this woman—a prisoner until he was twelve. His early environment was a dark, sick person's room. He was treated by his grandmother as a girl and his sexual identity molded by the restriction that he could play only with girls and with girl's toys. Even his vocabulary became one expected of females. He appears to have felt guilty masquerading as a male and hiding his underlying feelings of weakness while maintaining his male image with counterphobic (over-compensatory behavior). His spiritual guide became the Samurai Code of behavior, thus simultaneously controlling his hostility and masking his frailty.

Concealing his feelings from both mother and grandmother came at a substantial emotional cost—the repression of rage and the development of a sadomasochistic fantasy world. *Forest In Full Bloom* gives insight into Mishima's equation of beauty with the "ecstasy of death." He later wrote of "beauty's kamikaze squad," and his adolescent longing brought him into proximity with death as the supreme beauty. His emphasis on self-sacrifice was later clear in the autobiographical work *Confessions of a Mask.*

Prior to this novel, Mishima had known critical, but not popular success. *Confessions of a Mask* (*Kamen No Kokuhaku*), published in 1949, is an almost clinical description of the author and represents the "Rebel Without a Cause" of his day. Contemporaneously, Albert Camus wrote *The Stranger,* containing the same artistic elements.

Mishima portrays himself even at the age of five as a child with antipathy for reality and an immersion into sadism as a formidable defense against reality. His death was a death in fantasy devoid of the mundane, vulgar and loathsome aspects of the real battlefield. Nevertheless, *Confessions of a Mask* was a therapeutic effort—of literary and psychological survival. In 1948, as he wrote this novel, he likely had come to the understanding of the dangers of his flirtation and eventual entrenchment with fantasies of death and destruction.

The suicide of novelist Osamu Dazai in June 1948 was likely an important incident in this understanding. Dazai, the spokesman of his age, was a popular hero and Mishima understood his "glorification of despair." Mishima later wrote, "This was due to my immediate sense that Dazai was a writer at pains to expose precisely that which I most wanted to conceal in myself." Mishima began to locate his self-destructive impulses and projected them onto Dazai in an almost hateful fashion, which led to a personal confrontation that is now a famous incident in Japanese literary history. The terror of Mishima's own self-awakening was thus the instrument of his projective object.

All art is ultimately about death. In Yukio Mishima's case, life imitates art. This is true in the intensity and complexity of his daily existence and his choice of demise. Mishima was a man with closely cropped hair, the commander of his private army of 100 men, a man with a remarkable physique who, like Teddy Roosevelt, went from being a weakling to an athlete. Mishima was a man who could be the life of the party, yet a man who could be angry and hold grudges; a determined goal-directed obsessive man preoccupied with rituals and blood-signing oaths, a man remarkably traditional yet remarkably modern. He was a cult figure for some; a man who wanted to live forever. Yet, Mishima was a man who took his own life as a martyr of heroic Japan, a man who obeyed an order "that no earthly emperor was ever again going to give," a man who coveted the possibility of winning the Nobel Prize. Yet, in his moment of triumph, was preoccupied with the urge to destroy himself. All this, and more, was Mishima. Significantly, Mishima had visited Yasunari Kawabata on New Years Day in 1946. Kawabata had already written, *"From this point on, as one already dead, I intend to write only of the poor beauty of Japan, not a line else."*

In *Thieves,* written by Mishima in 1948, the hero learns he has been rejected for marriage and develops "this languorous suffering." His "discovery" that his longing for the girl has been converted to a longing for death emphasizes that he is not capable of a normal relationship.

There are two incidents which brought Mishima "closest to death" in the mid to late 1940s—to which he attributed his "brutal lyricism." The first was the death of his sister Mitsuko in October 1945. He wrote, "I loved my sister. I loved her to an inexplicable degree.... A few hours before her death, when she was quite delirious, I heard her say clearly, 'Brother, thank you,' and I wept." The biographer, John Nathan wrote in 1974, "Watching his sister die in such surroundings undoubtedly contributed to the morbid darkness which deepened in Mishima during these postwar years."

Mishima refers to the second incident less intensely, "There was another postwar incident in my personal life. A girl with whom I had associated during the war and to whom I would shortly have been engaged, because of my indecision, married someone else." The final third of *Confessions of a Mask,* written in 1949, is devoted to his relationship with Sonoko.

In this book, Mishima tries to experience normal passion with Sonoko, but feels nothing. The hero knows he is deceiving himself but maintains the pretense and, after refusing her family's urging for marriage, waits a full year and then meets her every few months for an hour or two. This "chimerical love like a gas" totally collapses when he is transfixed by the sight of a young man naked to the waist and forgets Sonoko's very existence. "At this instant something inside of me was torn in two with brutal force... I heard the structure which I had been building piece by piece...collapse miserably to the ground" His masquerade of normality was apparent to observers.

Reliving life in *Confessions of a Mask,* Mishima arrives at an awareness of his latent homosexuality and his inability to feel alive or experience passion except in his sadomasochistic fantasies. Indeed his first ejaculation (*ejaculato*) at age twelve was prompted by Guido

Reni's *Saint Sebastian.* As Mishima wrote, "The arrows have eaten into the tense, fragrant youthful flesh and are about to consume his body from within with flames of supreme agony and ecstasy." Of Sebastian he wrote, "And was not such a beauty as his a thing destined for death? ... His was not a fate to be pitied...a fate that might even be called radiant." Mishima speaks of Sebastian's martyrdom as setting him apart from ordinary men of the earth and thus of his own destiny.

In *Confessions of a Mask,* Mishima's experiences are *objectified,* but they are not just an artistic device. He is attempting to analyze the root source of his "nihilistic estheticism." The mask is not designed to hide—the mask of sexual perversion is an attempt by the author to discover his real face. Near the end of the novel the hero experiences the relief of hopelessness by his experience of heterosexual failure. Mishima recognizes the impossibility of his masquerade and utter hopelessness. Nathan noted, "What he wants, requires, is a definition, a diagnosis however hopeless, so that he will be able, in the most literal sense, to live with himself."

Mishima spoke of *Confessions* as a "last testament" to leave behind in the "domain of death"—a "closing of accounts." However, this process of self-discovery was an opening of accounts and a foretelling of the future. This novel is consistent with the intent of Japanese literature—to provide the reader with a means to develop in himself/herself "through an immersion in the text, an ability to intuit the deep realities of life as perceived by the author" as stated by J. Thomas Rimer, author of *A Reader's Guide to Japanese Literature,* published in 1988. From a psychoanalytic perspective we find that sadism, sexuality and blood become fused, and the artistic genius of Mishima expresses his self-perspective in 1958 as, "the martyrdom which lay in wait for him along the way; that this brand which Fate had set upon him was precisely the token of his apartness from all the ordinary men of the earth."

In 1965, Yukio Mishima was rumored to be a candidate for the Nobel Prize. However, in 1968 that honor was bestowed on Yasunari Kawabata, the first Japanese novelist to win that award. Kawabata called Mishima "the Japanese Hemingway.... A writer of his caliber appears only once every 200 or 300 years."

In late 1965, five years before his suicide, Mishima began *Sun and Steel* which was published in serial form. His conclusion, thus expressed, was that his life had been a quest for "the ultimate verification of existence." Words were no longer a substitute for reality and he decided that language and art were to blame for "eating reality away" and thus his had lost his sense of being alive—his existence. Muscle, as he described, became the "language of the flesh."

In *Sun and Steel*, published in book form in 1968, Mishima conceived of muscle as a proof of existence. Confronted with "lumps of steel" he wrote, "On that day began my close relationship with steel that was to last for ten years to come.... Little by little, moreover, the properties of my muscles came increasingly to resemble those of the steel. This slow development, I found, was remarkably similar to the process of education, which remodels the brain intellectually by feeding it with progressively more difficult matter...the process closely resembled the classical ideal of education.... The steel faithfully taught me the correspondence between the spirit and the body: thus, feeble emotions it seemed to me, corresponded to flaccid muscles, sentimentality to a sagging stomach, and over-impressionability to an oversensitive white skin. Bulging muscles, a taut stomach, and a tough skin, I reasoned, would correspond respectively to an intrepid fighting spirit, the power of dispassionate intellectual judgment, and a robust disposition." In this regard Mishima saw himself as above and beyond "ordinary people," as words came before the flesh and needed to manifest themselves in the language of the body.

Mishima wrote of a "romantic impulse towards death" requiring a strictly classical body as its vehicle. His reality could not be fulfilled until he met the necessary physical qualifications—"A powerful, tragic frame and sculpturesque muscles were indispensable in a romantically noble death." In *Sun and Steel*, Mishima wrote, "Longing at eighteen for an early demise, I felt myself unfitted for it. I lacked, in short, the muscles suitable for a dramatic death." Muscles for Mishima were the existence and works of art. Their function was the opposite of words. His dreams became his muscles as he planned a union of art and life, and pain became the "sole proof of the persistence of consciousness within the flesh, the sole physical expression of consciousness."

Positive acceptance of pain and his interest in physical suffering deepened as he acquired more muscle. He consolidates his thinking by stating, "For the cult of the hero is, ultimately, the basic principle of the body, and in the long run is intimately involved with the contrast between the robustness of the body and the destruction that is death.... *The thing that ultimately saves the flesh from being ridiculous is the element of death that resides in the healthy, vigorous body; it is this, I realized, that sustains the dignity of the flesh.*"

The "reality that stares back at one" is death. The author has accounted for his actions—past, present and *future*. His "proof of existence" would only come with death. Death is the ultimate endorsement to the proof of his existence. This is the full expostulation of the "death esthetic" of his adolescence.

Henry Scott Stokes, author of *The Life and Death of Yukio Mishima,* noted that Mishima yearned to be a hero. He views the key to understanding *Sun and Steel* as Mishima's definition of tragedy—a privileged nobility finding its basis in physical courage and keeping the "average" at a distance. By sunbathing and weightlifting Mishima developed the attributes of the warrior and arrived at the romantic death of a samurai. "Thanks to the sun and the steel, I was to learn the language of the flesh, much as one might learn a foreign language...an aspect of my spiritual development."

Early in life, Mishima loathed his body, put all his efforts into literature and sought a second language. Developing his body was his alternative to literature; the "true antithesis of words." Art and Action. But he had to die while his body was still beautiful—and while he remained comparatively young—the definition of his suicide.

To understand Mishima, one must have some knowledge of Shinto, the indigenous religion of Japan. The word *Shinto* means "the way of the gods" or "the way of the sacred." Shinto claims a continuous existence pre-dating Christianity. Both Buddhism and Confucianism greatly stimulated the development of Shinto practice in Japan, especially from the perspective of ancestor worship and the aristocratic moral code that has been so important in Japan's political and social development through its entire history. The ethical obligations of Buddhist practice, as well as nature worship, are cornerstones of Shintoism—but not the whole story.

Most significant is that the Sun God, Shinto, is an integral part of the *Creation Myth of Japan*, not unlike the creation myths of other cultures. Thus, the development of Japan, with all its later implications of political unification, was integrally related to the "original" religion of Japan. The creation myth established a royal line which became the core of Shinto tradition and belief, becoming dominant in all institutions in Japan, especially in education where it established a close alliance with militarism. The result included the divine relationship between the Emperor and his people, with the Emperor being the living incarnation of the gods who founded Japan. It was Shintoism that General Douglas MacArthur, Supreme Commander of the Allied Powers in Japan, disestablished while voiding its legal rights.

On January 1, 1946, by an imperial edict, the Emperor renounced claims to divinity and declared that ties to the throne and the people depended on mutual trust and affection. This act horrified Mishima, who began to grasp the materialistic decay of Japanese civilization.

Up to this time, Shinto priests were *de facto* government officials. It was the unity of religion, government and militarism that MacArthur wished to abolish and that Mishima wished to return to. (Beginning with the Sino-Japanese War, 1894-1905, the Japanese government followed an "expansionist policy" and from that time until the end of World War II, State Shinto was manipulated by the militarists and nationalists as a spiritual weapon for "mobilizing the Nation to guard the prosperity of the Throne and the Empire."

Mishima advocated the unity of religion and government and Emperor worship—an Emperor cult. Psychoanalytical study and developmental information are not enough to understand this man (or any significant figure) in the absence of cultural, political and religious influence. Mishima himself was quite critical of Western scholars in the field of Japanese studies. His death in the office of the commanding general of the Eastern Army was the result of careful planning and commitment to intense religious and philosophical ideals.

In addition to the hero of *Patriotism*, the protagonist of *Run Away Horses*—a man who was a right-wing terrorist, also commits hara-kiri. In 1969, Mishima took the feature role in the film *Hitogiri*, and played the part of the man who rips open his stomach. His death rehearsals were both repetitive and ideological. Mishima had posed for a series of photographs for Kishin Shinoyama. In one, he posed as Saint Sebastian—the image that had inspired his first ejaculation. Suspended by a rope, three arrows pierce body. In *Death of a Man (Otoko no Shi)*, there are a number of poses in which he commits hara-kiri.

Mishima's writings, and his life and death all reflect the fusion of his aggressive and libidinal drives. For him, blood was beauty and represented the ultimate orgasm. His suicide was both culturally motivated and idiosyncratic. The Nobel Prize in Literature, awarded to Yasunari Kawabata, was a narcissistic defeat for Mishima, who spent his life compensating for underlying feelings of weakness and femininity. Having spent the first twelve years of his life in his grandmother's sickroom, he was immersed in sickness and death. Yukio Mishima's death in the Samurai manner allowed the expression of his hostile and sadomasochistic wishes in a culturally acceptable manner. He also avoided the ultimate body decay that comes with age; the decay he so despised.

Some authors, such as J. Yamamoto and M. Igo, who wrote the article "Japanese Suicide: Yasunari Kawabata and Yukio Mishima" which appeared in the *Journal of the American Academy of Psychoanalysis 3* in 1977, hypothesized that Mishima's suicide was an act of *restitution* creating a sense of male identity. His male identity issues were complicated by his lack of a close relationship with his father, Azusa.

In fact, Mishima wrote at night (throughout his entire life) so that his father would not be aware of what he was doing. He showed his manuscripts only to his mother, who saw to it each night that writing supplies were available. Even after his marriage, he greeted his mother first after returning home and kept his childhood *transitional objects* in close proximity. Mishima never came to terms with his father, and this is reflected in the patricide within his novel *The Sailor Who Fell From Grace With The Sea.* In this book, the father is destroyed and the mother is kept.

Confessions of a Mask reflects both the repression of true feeling and the idea of leading the life of a "mask" as well as the attempt to be "real" with a resultant intellectualization and creation of the "false self." In *Confessions*, there is also an attempt to accept his sexual feelings which had become obsessional.

Mishima's many rehearsals for death related to the cultural experiences of Japan, to actual incidents, and to his innate masochistic needs and desire to die for the internalized father "of old"—the Emperor—as well as the simultaneous destruction of his own internalized father. In this regard, there are similar psychodynamics to those of Mark Rothko (chapter 4). Thus, the destruction of the father in literary work and in reality also represented the longing for the father— a fantasy from his early childhood. By destroying himself, he killed the father inside him thus "solving" his Oedipal conflict.

His association of beauty—ecstasy—with death is long-standing and sexually prominent in his writings and in his life. Eventually, he desired the sunlight to replace his romantic penumbra and wrote in *Sun and Steel* of his need to find expression in ways other than the artistic—expression through the "language" of the body. He desired a method of integrating the "words" he created with the "real" world—an existence of consciousness.

Yukio Mishima's death involved multiple functions: to become a man—a male person; to die for a loved father (the Emperor); to "kill" the (real) father (internalized); to experience the ecstasy of death with its total representation of blood, pain, sexual excitement and cultural identification; and to "solve" the Oedipal struggle of his life.

In November 1970, after berating a group of soldiers he insisted be assembled, he committed *sepukku*—ritual suicide, an act for which he had rehearsed his entire artistic life.

6

A LION AMONG WOMEN: HELEN HARDIN

> *"Zeus has made you a lion among women,*
> *and given you leave to kill any at your pleasure."*
> – From the Homeric epic quoted in
> Baring & Cashford
> "The Myth of the Goddess: Evolution of an Image"

Alexandria David-Neel was born in Paris in 1868. She lived more than one hundred years (1868-1969) and is best known as an intrepid explorer of Tibet, the author of more than forty books, and for being a Buddhist scholar. Her life's journey was spiritual, culminating in her invitation into the secret practices of Tibetan Buddhism. She was an individualist who moved beyond social and family barriers to pursue her own spiritual quest and she became the first European to penetrate Tibetan mysteries.

A world away in another culture a different kind of woman followed her own iconoclastic patterns. This Native American woman enmeshed herself in an *internal idiosyncratic* search that proved to be remarkably creative and shocking. She too broke the barriers of tradition and the constraints of cultural norms and propriety. She penetrated, exposed and displayed the secrets of her people which some believe led to her ultimate destruction.

Helen Hardin was born in Albuquerque, New Mexico on May 28, 1943. Her father, Herbert Hardin, an Anglo security guard and her mother, Pablita Velarde, cherished their first born and gave her the Indian name Tsa-Sah-Wee-Eh (Little Standing Spruce). Her mother, an internationally recognized artist, was a full-blooded Santa Clara Pueblo Indian. When I think of Helen Hardin, I think of Spirit People— *Kachinas*—and Cloud People, and mysticism. I think of her pain, her oppositional nature, her vulnerability, her sense of responsibility and directness, and her artistic industry. Not that these descriptions encompass her persona. Hardin cannot be categorized in a neat package. All art is an internal projection of the artist—the pain, the joy, the conflicts and the mysteries.

Helen Hardin, abused both as a child and adult, reflected these experiences in her oeuvre. Her mother, Pablita, placed her own career above the demands of her children and was ambivalent about her daughter's choice of art as a pursuit. Pablita was also envious of Hardin's success and independence.

Art historian Jay Scott noted in his book, *Changing Woman: The Life and Art of Helen Hardin*, that Hardin never recovered from her mother's coldness. Perhaps this is why some of her hatreds were unreasonable. Scott wrote that Hardin wanted success, but not as an Indian woman painter. On the other hand, she remained close to her heritage. She told LouAnn Faris Culley, an art history professor, that despite her urban background and her view that American Indian art was growing away from tradition, "this doesn't stop me from wanting to express my Indian self. I see beauty in many things my cousins living traditionally on the reservation take for granted. I apply them in a new way, non-traditionally." More importantly, as Hardin's second husband, Cradoc Bagshaw, noted, she retreated into Indian spirituality; "Where she lived was really in her paintings."

Hardin was always on the edge. Her first marriage was to a white man. She painted *kachinas.* And, she asserted an individuality that was anathema to the Pueblo culture of her day. Her heritage was everything to her—and she painted the "real thing"—the projections of her internal identity. As her work matured, Hardin moved away from detail towards greater simplification and emphasis on basic shapes. Her struggles with cultural acceptance and the white man's prejudice resulted in obstinacy and perseverance that served her survival and artistic production.

For Carl Jung, the circle was the symbol of psychic wholeness—a symbol that became basic for Hardin and a reflection of her identity. For her, as Jay Scott notes, the circle was life itself. She painted the masks of the *kachinas*—the masks worn during sacred ceremonies by the Hopi and Pueblo Indians in Arizona and New Mexico.

Her preschool years were spent at Santa Clara Pueblo in New Mexico and her first language was Tewa. At the age of six she moved to Albuquerque with her family and learned English. She thus was never initiated into a clan which influenced her wide stylistic spectrum and preference for the abstract.

Helen Hardin went beyond the traditional work of The Studio at Santa Fe Indian School. She studied at a special program conducted by the University of Arizona, and went on to enroll at the University of New Mexico, majoring in Art History and Anthropology. Later, she attended the Special School for Indian Arts at the University of Arizona. From early childhood she was interested in making pictures, but likely did not want to consider entering into competition with her mother. The attitude was mutual.

When Hardin, early in her career, was asked to consider exhibiting her work at Coronado Monument, which was believed to have been inhabited by the prehistoric Anasazi (A.D. 1300-1600), her mother was so upset, she locked up all Helen's Indian clothes in a trunk and told her to borrow clothes for the event. The antagonistic mother-daughter relationship continued throughout Hardin's life and was characterized by intense competitiveness, jealousy, and lack of maternal warmth. The later was complicated by her mother's heavy drinking.

Hardin's individualism and personal artistic expression was also a threat to the traditional Pablita Velarde who reflected the ideas of her Tewa Pueblo in Santa Clara. Helen responded, "I had decided to be Anglo socially and Indian in my art," and she exhibited in opposition to those close to her. She said, "I decided I wanted to be an artist when I knew I would not have live in the shadow of my mother.

Hardin became a Catholic during her childhood, apparently because her mother had promised her father that this would be forthcoming. However, Hardin was torn and ambivalent about her religion—another dichotomy in her personality. She did, however, accept one religion—Catholicism—as her own once she dealt with the maternal underpinnings and rebelled. "…everything the nuns told us was bullshit."

Cradoc Bagshaw, her second husband, said much later, "Helen bypassed the "bullshit" of a decadent religion and communicated directly with her gods." He referred to Hardin's Indian religion and her preoccupation with painting *kachinas*—the intermediaries responsible for crops and pragmatic life expectations. *Kachinas* are "the invisible forces of life—not gods, but rather intermediaries, messengers" as described in the *Book of the Hopi*.

Revealing the exact configurations of these *kachina* masks outside the Pueblo is forbidden. They are between two worlds—heaven and earth—and Hardin painted them as Cloud People—her vision of God. "The *kachinas* are not real to the tribe but are real in my own mind," she explained. Hardin identified with these images and interestingly, her mother said after Hardin's death, "Helen may have got cancer because she painted *kachinas.*"

This comment is indicative of her mother's rejection of the fundamental basis of Hardin's identity; an identity undermined by two specific childhood experiences. The first was Hardin's weight problem. She was considered fat by her schoolmates, a circumstance that fully undermined her self-esteem and confidence. The other was the physical abuse at the hands of her mother, a situation complicated by the parental divorce when Hardin was 13. Hardin was devastated when she learned, from her mother, that her father was having an affair. This was especially hard because Hardin had been his favorite. Nevertheless, she remained close to him and he was later instrumental in helping her escape from her first marriage.

Although overweight as a child, Helen matured into an attractive woman. Her features gave the impression of softness yet her fine facial contour framed large eyes and dark hair. Men were naturally attracted to her. She could deliver diatribes and was known to many as a "bitch." She arbitrarily disliked some people for little or no reason.

Helen's marriage was abusive and certainly more painful and restrictive than her relationship with Pablita had ever been. Whereas Pablita was physically abusive and intensely controlling, Hardin's relationship with her husband, Pat Terrazas, was even worse. Terrazas hid her paints—prohibiting her artistic expression, and controlled her every movement. Hardin ended up leading a secret "double life" during her first marriage, and attempted to seek refuge from her mother. However, Pablita continued the physical beatings of Hardin even during Hardin's escapes from her husband. Margarete, Hardin's daughter, witnessed not only her father beat her mother, but watched her grandmother do the same. On one occasion, Pablita used a towel rack to strike Hardin and left a substantial permanent scar.

Finally, Helen Hardin was able to escape to Bogata, Colombia where her father was temporarily working. After six months she returned home a much stronger and more determined person. This trip helped her individuate and separate herself psychologically from her mother. She had matured artistically and had a successful exhibit in that country. She developed professional confidence as a result, having sold twenty-seven of her paintings at the United States Embassy.

She also developed a determination to be more directive of her own life and took an apartment in secret to avoid her husband (Terrazas), who continued to harass her. Her daughter lived with her. In the truest sense, to borrow Joseph Campbell's phrase, she completed a "Heroes Journey" and never really came home. She, more than ever, became her own person. She once said, "One needs to give (art) meaning. It's like life—one gets out of it what one puts into it."

With her return from Colombia, Hardin was featured on the cover of *New Mexico Magazine* which carried a reproduction of her painting *Chief's Robes,* a painting that won first prize at the Inter-Tribal Indian Ceremonial in 1969. The article stated, "Here the Robe's designs, which represent a purely *abstract* and almost psychedelic use of color and design, predict her later, deliberate experiments…This painting was an important point of departure for her."

Hardin was clearly innovative and the magazine's focus of attention turned her world around. The cover title, "Tsa-Sah-Wee-Eh

Does Her Thing," started it all. Her popularity soared. She wrote, "Everyone wanted a painting by Helen Hardin. It was insane. Everyone wanted jewelry like I was wearing. A woman married to an art dealer wanted a Pueblo haircut like mine; there were lots of women who wanted to look like me... There were people coming into Enchanted Mesa wanting to buy a painting, wanting to buy the necklace, the earrings, the *concha* belt—they wanted the whole Helen Hardin kit. I've never been able to think like that."

Hardin knew that women were looking inward and outward attempting to harmonize their roles in two worlds and in 1976, when the Public Broadcasting System chose Hardin as the lone female painter in a series of documentary half-hours on Indian artists, she told the filmmakers she wanted her program to look "healthy and whole." This resulted in visits to Hardin's studio which was then in Puye Cliffs and they obtained brief footage of her family.

Hardin returned again and again to the theme that life is a circle and integration is important. She drew in the sand: "This is a circle that spirals inside itself. That's how my life goes. This circle spirals and has new parts and someday will be complete but is not complete yet. The happier I am, the better my painting is, the happier my family is, it goes in a big circle." She also treated her daughter lovingly and with great understanding—unlike her mother's treatment of her.

Helen's life work was to use the techniques of art: color, composition, and light combined with mythology and mysticism to depict—even restore—harmony in her life and in the universe. She obsessively pursued her craft with an all-encompassing vigor that dominated her life and persona. She *became* her work—her art.

Hardin's work reflected integration of animate and inanimate objects—a web of relationships all interrelated in what the *Book of the*

Hopi describes as "…a web of correlative obligations…that must function harmoniously for the…progression of all on that one…cosmic Road of Life." No easy task. Hardin stated, "A lot of my work has to do with Fantasy and Spiritual themes, with giving a spiritual message…it makes me happy when a painting does turn out to be very spiritual thing and it pleases me when people are touched by this."

An early influence on Hardin's art was Joe H. Herrera. "He was one of the very first contemporary Indian painters and, as a young girl, I was fascinated by his work even though he was criticized for having broken with tradition." Hardin went beyond Herrera however, in her use of metaphor. LouAnn Faris Culley stated, "The non-representational quality of her work is a process of her *own mind* rather than simply a function of the subject." She was also influenced by Herrara's spray and spotter technique. This was probably a prehistoric method of paint application and Herrara was the first contemporary painter to use the method. Hardin went on to develop her own sense of design and cultural interpretation. Hardin also acknowledged the influence of photography on her composition. Her second husband, Cradoc Bagshaw, was a professional photographer.

Some of Hardin's works involved the application of twenty-five layers of iridescent acrylic paint overlaid with gold dust meticulously and compulsively applied. Her application of neon-esque liquids (metallic acrylics) on a crystalline acrylic base epitomized her ability to depict a sophisticated theological conception of God—a deity represented as one with the painter and the cosmos; a departure from tradition and individualistic representation—a synthesis of traditional and geometric patterns. The symbolism of her paintings expressed both the thought and the mysticism and feeling of the religious experience. As Culley noted about Hardin's paintings, "They can speak to anyone who has ever had a spiritual experience, evoking the deities not of any particular religion, but of all religions."

Sometimes Hardin was influenced solely by sounds—a recording of an Indian chorus singing, for instance. This was clearly innovative and creative iconography, ignoring commercial imperatives and integrating elements—such as figure and ground—in a technically sound and intensely communicative fashion. Hardin told Culley, "Rather than painting a subject, I am inspired by that subject to paint *what I feel from the idea*, the song, the ceremony, the mask. I paint it as I *feel* it rather than as I see it... This is what separates me from traditional painters who paint the actual object or scene. Traditional painting usually tells a story—contemporary art leaves you with a feeling rather than a story."

Jay Scott quotes LouAnn Faris Culley as saying Hardin succeeded in convincing the viewer that her paintings were a metaphor that could be deciphered, not with outside sources, but *within the painting itself.* This allows for a universal expression of religious-spiritual experiences. She created new forms that became "compelling metaphors." Both the unconscious and conscious latent mysticism manifestly communicate with the viewer. Jay Scott wrote this produces "a harmonious, evocative whole, regardless of the viewer's background." This, in spite of a mother who, in Hardin's words, "Expected so much out of me and so little from me."

Culley wrote, "Hardin's more personal metaphors draw the viewer into the painting and call fourth associations with not only the artist's background and experiences, but the *viewer's experiences as well*" (emphasis added). Hardin said, "Everything I do is made to be lived with but I want it to be aesthetically pleasing...I can produce a good, strong painting, and that's the goal I've set for myself."

Throughout the 1970s, Helen Hardin worked feverishly for long hours consuming substantial amounts of caffeine. She was eventually medicated with antidepressants and ultimately had a "breakdown" necessitating admission to Bernanillo County Mental Health Hospital where she was hospitalized for one month and then treated as an outpatient for nine months. Working enormously hard, raising her daughter Margarete alone, having no social life, being in the pressured relationship with her mother, and her problematic first marriage, was an environment that all began to close in on her. Her marriage to Bagshaw, however, changed all this.

She met Cradoc Bagshaw a few weeks after her psychiatric hospitalization and although "all the men I met turned out to be liars," he was obviously different and even adopted Margarete. The three of them became "fused at the hip." Bagshaw helped Hardin stand up for what she believed in and gave her confidence. Hardin grew emotionally and artistically and further distanced and distinguished herself from the opportunism of commercially-motivated Indian art. Hardin's marriage to Bagshaw in 1973 was an enormous boost to her self-confidence and ended the sporadic beatings from her mother who was, by this time, drinking one-fifth of whiskey a day. The "break" with her mother—which started years before—was complete. Hardin was finally free to transform Indian myth into *modern metaphor*. The iconographic significance of her work was reflected *universality*.

As Hardin matured as an artist, she became more risqué and playful but never less creative or meticulous. Some dealers fought her professional growth and others were uncomfortable with the overt sexuality expressed in some of her work. She finely tuned her attention to geometry and even likened her interest in geometrical designs to her love of the Catholic Church—ritual, designs, and structure.

Interestingly, in this regard, Hardin did not do preliminaries—she worked directly without sketches—directly from her creative imagination and was able to express the "deeply idealistic spirituality" of her soul. She created a balance between man's spiritual and physical natures.

As Jay Scott wrote, "Hardin was pursuing not only technical perfection, but its *spiritual* concomitant—her art was a record of her involvement with a universe in which man was depicted, in Artistole's phrase, "as he might and ought to be...a vision simultaneously Aristotelian and Jungian...she was profoundly alienated from the artistic mainstream."

As Hardin said of herself, "It's more important, finally, for people to like my art than to like me." She departed from the traditional to depict the mystical, being always on "the outside looking in" and never fully integrated her social-artistic identity as far as her community was concerned. She lived on the edge. The artistic expressions of her work include a geometry subservient to an underlying emotion. Her work, *Changing Woman,* has been said to be a map of the psyche integrating, in Scott's words, "...an unknown into an unknowable future." She was also expressing her own feelings—her own "self."

Hardin's identity evolved—a product of continuous transition of unconscious process. Here, once again, we see the application of the transitional object. This is a judgmental construct in the creative process. Her representations of women in her *Woman* series is dramatic and substantial. Women are feeling and *thinking* beings, not just "big boobs." One notes the "active anguish and covert ecstasy" described by Scott. *Listening Woman* has absorbed the sorrows of the universe and represents the timelessness of grief and stoicism. Again we find the interior, the depth, the unconscious. According to Scott, *Changing Woman, Listening Woman* and *Medicine Woman* represent "everything she got out of life." Likewise, in *Recurrence of Spiritual Elements*, we find that her complexity with design has been used in a *drive metaphor* and, according to Culley, "on the one hand it reflects *her own state of mind* at the time, having been done during a period of self-examination. On the other hand, the painting has a *general* spiritual message for the viewer."

Helen could be quite acerbic and self-determining. During her mature painting period she was able to promote herself and realistically price her paintings without pangs of guilt or remorse. One telling example of her memory and sense of self-identity occurred during an interview with Jay Scott. She reminded him that ten years prior to his interview with her, "...when you lived here, you covered the New Mexico Arts & Crafts Fair for *The Albuquerque Journal* and you came by my mother's booth and my booth. You wrote about her but you never wrote about me. Not once in the three years you covered the Arts and Crafts Fair did you ever mention me." She was right.

Hardin was honest and did not let things slide—she was direct and confrontive. As Jay Scott noted, she could not silence an inner voice that demanded the truth and this did make life more difficult for her. Being Native American—and a woman—she felt and expressed, "I try harder." Her task in art was to become life.

In October of 1981, Helen Hardin was diagnosed with breast cancer. In response, her painting became the increasing focus of her life. She spoke of the spirit and sense of comfort she took from *Medicine Woman*, although her weakness, suffering and pain continued. She dealt with the loss of body parts, keeping her feminine and personal identity intact, and continued painting after her mastectomy to produce the second in her "Intellectual Women' series. *Listening Woman,* the final work in the series, symbolized compassion.

122

Eventually, in spite of surgery, radiation and chemotherapy, Hardin developed a metastasis and recurrence of the tumor in 1983. Her paintings became even more spiritual, culminating in *Harmony Brings Gifts From The Gods*, her last great work. This painting was used as a poster for the 1983 New Mexico Arts & Crafts Fair. Helen Hardin had known almost from the start that her illness was incurable. Even then her mother spoke disapprovingly, "She's accepted the *penalty* of death," Pablita stated, as if Hardin deserved the illness and its ultimate consequences. Bagshaw said, "She just let go of life, finally." Helen Hardin died at home on June 9, 1984.

Clara Lee Tanner, an art historian, maintains that Hardin's art had reached full maturity at the time of her death. "Her work ran the gamut from delicate pastels to rich mixed media, from prehistoric to fantastic subject matter. She had moved from simple realism into fully geometric and abstract styles." She also noted that at the time of Hardin's death, she was "The top female Indian artist in the Southwest, if not the nation."

7

LOSS, RESTITUTION AND CREATIVITY: THE LIFE OF EDVARD MUNCH

"Ay, in the very temple of delight
Veiled Melancholy has her sovran shrine,
Though seen of none save him whose strenuous tongue
Can burst Joy's grape against his palate fine;
His soul shall taste the sadness of her might,
And be among her cloudy trophies hung."
     – John Keats
        "Ode on Melancholy"

The psychoanalyst Arnold Modell wrote, "The greatest danger to the human child is separation from the parents. However, the child fears not only the actual physical separation from the parents but also the instinctual demands he places upon the parents—demands which endanger his relationship to them will also result in anxiety...the mother is the child's earliest environment...the very conditions of excessive dependency lead to anxiety and the creation of a private inner world."

With "creative people" this inner magical world uses symbol formation to guarantee, in a psychological sense, the continued existence of love and security. One again we find that the *transitional object* becomes a substitute for the actual environment. This substitute protects the creator from the losses of the environment. The transitional object does exist in reality, separate from, yet connected to, the individual. The object, in a sense, is not separate from the person. For the artist, this transitional object becomes a symbol. A symbol in psychoanalytic terms represents something repressed and not expressed verbally. The artist has the ability (creative genius) to associate (usually unknowingly) to this repressed experience and represent it for the viewer-participant. There is then a resonance with the participant's unconscious (in the artistic experience).

In this regard, the transitional object preserves what is "lost" to consciousness (nothing is ever lost in the psyche). It is the connection between fantasy and reality and the expression of the inner experience. The early transitional object of the child becomes, in the hands of the creator, the creative experience manifested by *works of art*. In this regard we understand from the psychoanalyst D.W. Winnicott the concept of the *good enough mother* who allows the child to exist in a *holding environment* with nurturing and facilitating and who later allows the child to experience his own creativity. There is a "first-time-ever quality" to this new experience of the child and the same is true with the artist.

Helen Hardin (chapter 6) was able to create experiences similar to that expressed by European artists of another generation without ever knowing about them. The mother's external reality allows the child an experience to use his capacity to create. The artist then later creates and recreates reality—both representing the conscious and unconscious aspects of existence. The mother, in early development, may be thought of as a psychological "*mirror*."

Leonardo da Vinci (chapter 9) may have actually been painting his mother when he represented the *Mona Lisa* and recreated, as Freud noted, the early blissful experience with his mother. This memory is not the entire story nor is it the basic issue. The "holding" environment and adaptive qualities of the "good enough mother" allow the child to develop and experience *de novo*. The "good enough mother" provides an optimal opportunity for the child to experience and create. As time goes on the child expands beyond the maternal umbrella and this is also an experience of *loss.*

Psychological life has been described as *loss and fear of loss.* This is necessary and the maturing process creates a reality base. The artist has the ability to, in a sense, live in both worlds—the intrapsychic, and the reality worlds. Mentally ill people may do the same but they are not "creative" in the communicative sense nor can they distinguish the inner from outer reality—their "filtering" mechanism has broken down. A failure of infant-mother adaptation has taken place. The growing away of the individual from the mother has been described as a lifetime "mourning process" and it is the transitional object that helps the child progress beyond the maternal-infant relationship—the sense of "one-ness" with the mother to the individualized stage of personal identity and "sense of self." The artist is then able to create a connection between his inner and outer world. The transitional object helps maintain that which is lost and allows the transition to individuation. This experience allows a relationship between inner (psychic) and outer reality. In this regard, the transitional object has been said to be the prototype for later artistic experience. Psychologically speaking, it is "risky" to create. The early holding environment allows the child to develop the security and comfort for risk-taking in the truest (psychic) sense. We also see this in a healthy child's play. Artistic creativity may also be viewed as an extension of *play*—bridging the gap between inner and outer reality. Obviously there are artists whose early maternal environment was not a facilitating atmosphere. In these instances, we are confronted with the need for *restitution and repair*.

The artistic gifts evolve from the same intrapsychic experiences and the transitional object relationships, and also represent the development of what was missed in the available (maternal) relationship. Some artists' mothers were depressed, hostile, or dead. Some were simply indifferent or preoccupied with survival. The artistic products of these environments (the artists) compensate for the early deprivations by creative mechanisms that serve to "solve" the early experience of deprivation, pain or loss. The inner experience is communicated through works of art resonating with the "inner experiences" and losses we have all experienced, although perhaps with lesser intensity. The artist develops a *transference relationship* with his creation, projecting to the creative object his *intrapsychic experience* and "reworking," but never resolving, his earlier developmental traumas.

The Belgian artist Rene Magritte (1898-1967), lost his mother in his early adolescence when she committed suicide by drowning. Psychoanalyst Martha Wolfenstein studied this artist's visual imagery as related to the maternal loss. Wolfenstein described the improbability of resolving parent loss prior to adolescent maturation—a circumstance that leads to unresolved grief and later psychological and psychosomatic problems. In the artist's situation, he is communicating with non-verbal material—visual imagery. This imagery is a representation of *pre-verbal* experience in many, but not all, instances. One must understand, however, that there are multiple experiences of loss and, as I have previously explained, the initial "loss" of moving away from the mother and individuating. In Magritte's case, his birth was followed by the replacement of maternal possession with the birth of two siblings. The loss of the maternal "object" (the mother) at the age of thirteen had been preceded by previous psychological "traumas," including frequent moves from town to town and house to house. For Magritte, the continual reworking of themes in his paintings is characteristic of the artist's persistence in visual representation of psychological themes and issues of significance without ever "working through" or "solving" the original series of losses, unless there is an active psychological treatment. Magritte's art depicts representations of the experience of seeing his mother's naked body as she was taken from the water. His images, painting women partly alive and partly dead, and the association of inanimate symbolism, are characteristic of the inability to mourn the loss and the artist's maintenance of the painful memory— the persistence of the "early pain." There is also the issue of sexual symbolism in his paintings.

Magritte also developed an intense attachment to his wife, Georgette, whom he met shortly after his mother's death. Years later he married Georgette and vowed never to be separated from her. When she became ill shortly after their marriage he became extremely anxious but was able to sublimate this discomfort and fear to artistic creation. His paintings represent an attempt to "undo" the reality of his loss. His paintings "speak" to the viewer of his unresolved grief and pain. His sense of early emptiness and primitive memories of loss are depicted visually. The artist is dealing, as most artists do, with the issue of reality and illusion. Van Gogh (chapter 8) used color and pigment to do the same thing. The artist, Andrew Wyeth, (chapter 2) speaks of an "artistic honesty" in his approach to reality, all the while conveying his emotional tone and experience of both intrapsychic and cultural reality.

Generally, the artist is unaware of the experience of intrapsychic representation. Georgia O'Keefe is a good example of an artist who removed herself from any "interpretation" of her work on a psychological level, at least interpretations dealing with conflictual and instinctual drives. Perhaps this is necessary. As mentioned earlier, the symbol and artistic representation is a depiction of repressed material—material not readily available in consciousness. The symbol represents what has been repressed.

In the life and work of Edvard Munch we discover similar themes of loss and attempts at restitution but also learn of the intervention of psychiatric treatment. We learn something of the effect *treatment* has on the "creative process." A child or an adolescent has not developed the mastering capabilities to deal with the loss of a parent. In psychoanalysis we speak of "mastery functions" of the ego and use such terms as "executive function" or "capacity" when describing mastery issues. That is, mastery over conflict and loss. In Munch's case his art became the representation of his unresolved grief and the inner conflicts it generated.

Munch is perhaps Norway's greatest painter and printmaker. He is considered by many art historians as a father of German Expressionism. He as born in Engelhaug and raised first in Oslo, then in Christiana. His father was a military physician and was said to "suffer" from religious anxieties. During his childhood Munch's mother and older sister died from tuberculosis. These themes of death, disease and suffering are the obvious themes of his art.

Edvard Munch entered art school at age seventeen and eventually evolved a style and theme of depicting man as the object of overwhelming external forces. Man is helpless before the forces of life and death. Of main concern in his work is man's relationship to women. Women are often represented as idealized, erotic or what has been described as the "death-mother." Ultimately, man is destroyed by each. His self-portraits also represent inner torment.

Art in Germany around the turn of the century reflected the political nationalistic perspective of the government and was basically regionalized with isolated schools of art. Nationally, it was the function of artists to support and glorify national objectives and historical representation. However, German character trait set the stage for the development of Expressionism. Especially with Munch, the inner needs of the subject matter determined the forms of artistic productions.

Various "Secessions" rose during the 1890s in opposition to the establishment's art mentality. The first of them, in 1892 in Munich, the "Society Against the Association of Artists" was formed to raise the standard of exhibitions. By 1889 in Berlin, Max Liebermann became the head of the "Alliance of Eleven" which included progressive artists of all kinds. This group was enlarged, partly as a result of the work of Edvard Munch, and the Berlin Secession came into existence.

Although he participated in the Berlin exhibition in 1892, Munch's paintings were received with hostility. He was able to continue his work of expressing the emotional tone of his inner experience using, but not necessarily emphasizing, the literal nature of his work. He mastered etching and used the surface texture of woodblock. Some believe that his greatest artistic productions are his prints.

In 1902, this group exhibited twenty-eight paintings by Munch. Considered historically significant were the Munich Secession, the Dresden Secession, and new associations such as the Neu-Dachau group which was further subdivided into the older artists with their Germanic "tone-poems," and the younger artists—the "Clod Group" with their brighter, more striking use of color. And so this turn of the century artistic rebellion continued to sprout and was complimented by the development in Munich of the German Arts and Crafts Movement during the 1890s with its emphasis on craftsmanship.

The Munich influence spread throughout Germany. Munch's contribution to this movement was influenced by his experiences and associations with Van Gogh, Gauguin and Toulouse-Lautrec during his association in Paris. Likely, the influence of these other artists "sensualized" Munch's work. Both Toulouse-Lautrec and Munch used the outline and arabesque, with Munch expressing his sense of burden and psychological "angst."

The origin of the word "Expressionism" is not known, but it was first used in the catalogue of the twenty-second exhibition of the Berlin Succession in April 1911. The word "Expressionism" again appeared in connection with the Sonderbund exhibition held in Cologne in 1912 in a catalog discussion that describes "rhythm" and "colourfulness" to "simplify and intensify the forms of expression." The first monograph on the subject was prepared by Paul Fechter in Munich in 1914. He described Expressionism as a counter-movement against Impressionism. Fechter's description includes German avant-garde with "Dresden and Munich" as the birthplaces of the new art.

Wassily Kandinsky referred to Expressionism in his essay, "On The Spiritual In Art." He wrote, "...presenting nature not as an external phenomenon, but predominantly the element of the inner impression, which has recently been called Expression."

Franz Marc wrote that these "wild beasts" produced another goal, "the creation, through their work, of symbols for their age, which belong on the altars of the coming religion of the spirit, and behind which the technical creator disappears from sight." This new kind of art became "the symbol and expression of a new kind of human being." Robert Waelder, a psychoanalyst, describes expressionistic art as that which describes inner life, not visible realities. He writes in *Psychoanalytic Avenues to Art* of the "distortion of appearances" and contrasts it with Surrealism which he relates to the "realistic visual recording of dreams and fantasies. Expressionism and Surrealism are one in their intention, which is the expression of subjective states of mind without regard to objective, i.e., intersubjective, realities...the artist is particularly close to his Unconscious. The Unconscious manifests itself in his works without the artist himself necessarily knowing or fully comprehending what he is doing."

These products speak directly to the *Unconscious* of the spectator—a conversation from one person, the artist, to another, the viewer on a subliminal basis. Waelder goes on to say that this same experience is true of scientific pursuits and to some extent we can understand this through our study of Leonardo da Vinci (chapter 9) who used dream and fantasy material to create scientific objects externally represented. With the works of artists, this does not explain the creative aspect because the art itself must have some "control" to "make sense"—it is not just out-of-control fantasy. Otherwise it would not be art. According to Waelder, "The imagination of the artist has to be controlled by the ego." He notes the *fundamental* similarity between scientific pursuits and the arts and once again we find this combination with Leonardo da Vinci. In art this "...is the Unconscious of Jung, an archaic world common to all of us, or to all people of a race, a nation, or civilization—a realm through which man is supposed to communicate with the species, the Cosmos, and the Absolute."

Edvard Munch, who was born in 1863 and died in 1944, was an intensely introspective man preoccupied with suffering, loneliness and, at times, despair. In his mature years he became preoccupied with jealousies, drank too much and fought with his contemporaries. His internal "angst" became externalized and personified. He was not an "easy" person to get along with and would not have been "liked" by contemporary Americans.

Early on, in 1890 while in France, Munch formulated a goal that became a relentless obsession—acting as a prophet or priest. He said of his paintings, "People would understand the sacredness of them and take their hats off as if in church." He committed himself to humanism driving himself in the belief in the power of art to communicate truths of existence to *ordinary people.* No doubt this obsessional drive related to the deaths of his mother and later his sister from tuberculosis. His young years were profoundly disturbed by those experiences and complicated by the aggressiveness of his father who appeared, by all accounts, to suffer from severe anxiety and religious delusions—a man described "to have come close to religious dementia."

As a student, Munch was involved with a radical, questioning group of writers and settled on his artistic themes—the intense expression of inner states of the mind, specially the suffering mind, and man and woman relationships. Munch compulsively worked and reworked the themes of his early childhood. He especially focused on loneliness.

In Edvard Munch we have the image of an intensely compulsive, lonely man haunted throughout his life and unable to find refuge except in his artistic pursuits. He spoke to his paintings, treated them like people and refused to put them up for sale. They became his reliable people substitutes. Van Gogh's and Gauguin's philosophy, as well as their formal innovations, influenced him greatly. The flowing colors, the distortion of form, the juxtaposition of bright contrasting colors became hallmarks of the works of these men. Munch never abandoned the *inner needs* of the subject matter, and these needs shaped the outer form of his work.

Munch overwhelms with the intensity of his inner experiences. By 1908 he had become famous not only in Norway and Germany, but internationally as well. It was in 1908 that his "psychology" caught up with him. His love affairs, drinking and fighting resulted in his "nervous collapse" and he withdrew to the sanitarium of Dr. Jacobsen at Copenhagen. Munch summed up his work in art in six words: *"I hear the scream in nature."* He painted from "the hopeless conviction of man's aloneness in the world, his vulnerability to misfortune and spiritual violation." The sense of isolation and aloneness occurs even in the context of relationships. In *Anxiety,* Munch established individuals trapped by their sense of isolation and spiritless. "The pale staring eyes see nothing." *Art nouveau,* with its emphasis on the rhythms of lines of natural forms to achieve the effects of isolation and loneliness, is an inheritance from Munch. This free distortion of form and color helped give rise to the disclosure of inner states and emotions.

The new developments in the use of color during the Fauvist movement were enhanced in the Expressionist movement with the connotations of pathos and tragedy, although Fauvism is a form of Expressionism. For Munch, he—and man—is a victim!

Munch developed an unresolved grief reaction as a result of the losses of his mother and sister. As with any child or adolescent, he could not deal with these catastrophic losses of his childhood. After his mother's death he became emotionally dependent on his sister, only to lose her as well. He investigated the themes of death, loneliness, jealousy and love, not only in his paintings but in his drawing and prints as well, establishing himself as a great printmaker. Munch anticipated many of the later advances in lithographs and he used woodcuts to achieve his stark message. These woodcuts had a profound impact on Expressionism and cannot be overlooked—not just because of the technical skill—but because of the success of communication they provide. Art is a form of communication sometimes used to master feelings and conflict, but Munch never achieved this mastery. Visual expression allows the artist to represent layers of meaning condensed, as in a written poem. Past and present experiences of an his inner life can be depicted through art. A painting becomes a synopsis of beauty.

Munch attempted to use the visual media to uncover and exper-ience his anger, guilt and despair. These feelings, never mastered in childhood, were also not mastered in his adult life in spite of the great success of the artist's work itself. His nervous breakdown in 1908 resulted from these unresolved issues manifesting themselves by feelings of persecution, conflicts and fighting with friends, excessive alcohol consumption, preoccupation with anxieties and memories, and depression. These events were the culmination of years of problematic experiences.

He was a suspicious man with strong ambivalence regarding sexuality and women. This relates to this unresolved maternal longings and the themes of this ambivalence reoccurs throughout his life and his work. *The Androgynous Madonna* (1909) is a *self*-portrait with breasts representative of his maternal identification.

There are many perspectives to take when attempting to understand parent loss in childhood, including the idea that children deny the loss of the parent to avoid a response to this loss. This is a psychological denial that frequently results in an identification with the lost parent. Children are unable to engage in mourning. The loss is too threatening and the denial is psychological. Childhood loss also interferes with the later development of relationships and the capacity to love. The relationship patterns these individuals "act out" as adults represent patterns stemming from the relationship to the dead parent. In this way, just as the child "identified" with the lost parent, the child "compensates" for the loss. The individual in this situation suffers from diminished self-esteem, may overly idealize the dead parent, and may also develop symptoms that mimic the parental identification.

In Munch's situation, he suffered from a lifelong series of upper respiratory illnesses and evidenced all of the sequellia of pathological grief. The major task of mourning is "giving up" what has been, in reality, lost, but this is not accomplished in pathological mourning. Through treatment, we help adults to do the work of mourning by continuous reality testing, remembering, and by comparing then and now. The child cannot do this outside a therapeutic situation. When this work of "giving up" is not accomplished, the adult remains unable to complete the work of mourning and he resists giving up the lost parent.

Munch's art clearly reveals the symptoms of unresolved grief reaction although he "attempted" to work through these losses with his artistic endeavors. It is as if he wanted to experience and re-experience the feelings associated with his losses. He obsessively reworked his subjects and themes to this purpose. The master, however, was never accomplished. Instead, we are left with the wonder and greatness of his attempts—his artistic accomplishments. *They speak to our losses—our own anxieties—our loneliness—our desolation—our sense of detachment.* The value of the work is its communication *to our psyche.* Munch himself spoke of his pain, "...disease and insanity were the black angels on guard at my cradle. In my childhood I felt I always was treated in an unjust way, without a mother, sick, with threatened punishment and hell hanging over my head.... *My art has allowed me to bare my soul.*"

Munch was able to recreate these experiences in images—a product of the inexplicable artistic genius of his nature. "In the reflection about this and in the release through my art lay a need to and a wish that my art may bring me light." In his 1890 drawing *Outside the Gate,* one finds a young boy holding his mother's hand as she stands in the dark doorway—in the shadow. His 1890s painting *Dead Mother with Spring Landscape* also expresses the association of life and death. *The Dead Mother* is another work of similar theme. In *The Scream,* we find his protest and reaction to his mother's death. The ears are covered—there is terror and anxiety—deep pain. *The Sick Child*, done in 1886, likely represents his sister Sophie's illness and he wrote of "...the last cry of pain" associated with this painting. *By the Deathbed* and *Death in the Sick Chamber* have similar associations with Munch vicariously experiencing his sister's suffering.

Munch was five years old when his mother died from tuberculosis. His response was to develop a close attachment to his sister Sophie, but she died when he was thirteen. Once again we find a series of losses compounded by other external circumstances influencing the inability to experience grief.

Munch's father was emotionally unavailable to him and the boy was psychologically abandoned. No wonder we find Munch's adult behavior and relationships characterized by jealousy and fear (of loss). The father's psychiatric disorder and depression further complicated the childhood experience and, somewhat like the writer Yukio Mishima (chapter 5), Munch was surrounded by sickness and death. These traumas were exacerbated by poverty. Edvard Munch had three younger siblings, including one sister who developed a serious psychiatric illness and spent much of her life in hospitals. Not surprisingly, none of Munch's self-portraits depict him smiling. Rather, we see a despondent individual;

lost and alone. *The Sick Child,* done when he was 22 years old, is considered his first major work. It recalls the scene of his dying sister. He painted this picture *six times* during the course of his life and experienced grief again and again in reworking this experience. *The Scream* clearly represents loss—of self, of life and of his family. He also reproduced this picture many times throughout his life.

Even in his romantic life Edvard Munch recapitulated his family constellation. He developed a six-year obsession with a married woman who resembled his mother and *whose husband was a physician like Munch's father.* He describes this relationship in damaging and destructive terms, almost blaming the woman for his misery. He later *repeated* the experience with a painful attachment to the wife of another artist. Ultimately, with still another female entanglement, he was involved in an accidental shooting resulting in the loss of two joints off one finger on his left hand. This created physical as well as emotional pain, again providing Munch with an external object to blame for his suffering. He developed considerable distrust of women around these relationships. He was able, however, to depict the experiences in his paintings. *Death and the Maiden,* done in 1893, depicts a woman embracing a skeleton. *Vampire* evidences a woman's head buried in a man's neck. The message is that women are both threatening and dangerous. In *Harpy,* a birdlike woman tears a man apart. In *Women With A Brooch* (1903), the model, Eva Muddocci, resembles his mother. *Salomé* (1903) depicts the image of a woman as a murderous object.

The women in Munch's life could not replace his relationship with his dead mother. They were poor substitutes at best; dangerous and destructive at worst. His longing to be reunited with his mother is characterized by the repeated paintings of her—an attempt to reestablish the lost relationship. In similar fashion he recreated his sister and father many times. Importantly, with the loss of his mother, repressed hostility was transferred to other relationships, especially with women. This destructive *repetition compulsion* resulted in repeated abandonment by the object of his love and the unfulfillment of his inner needs. He painted the destructiveness and hostility and acted it out as well. Women are vampires draining men. Women are interpreted as innocent in *Separation;* threatening and dangerous, or withdrawing of love and attachment.

In 1908 Munch was treated at Professor Daniel Jacobson's psychiatric clinic and, in addition to working on his alcohol problem, he began to confront the psychological traumas of his life. Hospitalization in Copenhagen followed the death of two close friends. His therapy included the uncovering and working through of painful childhood experiences. Munch developed a positive relationship with the doctor and his staff and benefited greatly from the eight months of treatment. He painted a substantial portrait of his doctor, experiencing this relationship with an ideal paternal object (father figure). It was an immensely important experience leading to his cure. He went on to complete a major work—a series of lithographs illustrating a prose poem "Alpha and Omega." The work offered a partial resolution of his own conflict by externally representing abandonment, betrayal and punishment. He "objectified" his own anxiety about punishment. Munch wrote, "A strange calm came over me while I was working on the series, as if all malice had left me."

At age forty-five Munch became a changed man. His relinquishment of the "lost objects" of his childhood—his mother and sister— was probably not complete, but it was complete enough to change the character of his work forever. Critics generally agree that his profoundly original and creative work occurred before 1908 and that the work of his later years appears to have lost its intensity and meaning. Intuitively Munch realized his art was dependent on conflicts arising from his grief, and he wrote about this. He, however, experienced an "inner change" after his hospitalization and treatment and his return to Norway.

Here we have the situation where psychiatry had a major influence on the artistic creations of an individual "dependent" on his neurosis for creativity. In *Vampire* and *Madonna,* woman is realized as both creator and destroyer, yet in his later years Munch developed a freer and lighter style with less emphasis on the subject matter of his earlier works. One finds, however, in S*elf-Portrait Between Clock And Bed* a continued vestige of his loneliness and desolation. A man perhaps waiting for time to run out; waiting to die. The inner needs of his subject matter still found expression in this work.

In later years he developed an even more intense relationship to his paintings and treated them as if they were living people. He even called them his children and avoided selling them or parting with them. It was as if they replaced his relationships with people. As with Van Gogh, the paintings became his children; perhaps he could reduce his feelings of anxiety and envy towards women by the "experience" and fantasy of giving birth through his children—his paintings. Van Gogh wrote about this openly and Munch lived the fantasy openly. He could give birth and nurture. He could feel more comfortable around his artwork. He was assured of immortality, especially by 1909 when he received the Order of St. Olaf from Norway. His art was reparative in the sense that he contributed, perhaps lessening his guilt for "imagined responsibility" over the childhood losses. His creativity was an attempt to deal with loss, punishment, guilt, grief and loneliness. His art was an attempt to undo the dread of loss of love. Munch wrote, "I should not want to reject my illness because my art owes a great deal to it."

Munch's fantasized reunion with his mother was accomplished through his art work and later in therapy with the actual, although partial, resolution of his pathological grief. His creative product symbolized his needs and fantasies. His artwork was most likely a manifestation of the transitional object—the symbolization of his inner experience. He externalized the work of mourning with the symbol—the artwork—that was both a transitional object and a *linking object*. That linking object, a term described by Vamik Volkan, describes the object, in this case art, that allows a transition and a "link" to deeper more relevant "objects" and experiences—from the psyche to the "external world." Munch's early traumatic loses influenced all of his close relationships, especially his romantic associations. By depicting his inner (psyche) experiences with his creative expression (art), he ultimately mastered much of his conflict. In doing so, he speaks to our unconscious since his life's themes and personal experiences are universal.

Munch's creativity has given us an avenue to appreciate and experience similar feelings and desires. And perhaps his art helps in our understanding of mortal existence and life's meaning.

8

LIVING WITH A GHOST: VINCENT VAN GOGH'S LEGACY

"...we will eat our meal in fear, and sleep
In the affliction of these terrible dreams,
That shake us nightly: better be with the dead...
Than on the torture of the mind to lie In restless ecstasy."
–Shakespeare
"Macbeth"

Some art historians believe that Vincent Van Gogh's work has survived, indeed penetrated our psyche, because he painted the deepest fears and wishes of mankind—something that is of universal unconscious appeal. Van Gogh's life was one of unprocessed pain. He escaped from the limits of linear logic to created in the transitional realm of inner experience and external life. His childhood experiences served as internal objects generating an independent reality that we can all, at some fundamental level, understand. We, as observers, find the unfamiliar in the familiar. Van Gogh retained the transitional space of the childhood he intensely experienced and transformed that experience to an object of external reality and, simultaneously to an "object" of internal reality.

In our study of pathography we may treat the artistic work as if it were a *dream* and also treat the artistic work and the artist as if they were patients on the couch. In dreams we *displace* feelings from one object or person to another less emotionally "loaded" one. We *condense* images and symbols and we use defense mechanisms to produce an image that is acceptable, one that allows us to continue sleeping. By using these defense mechanisms and symbols we produce a *creation* that communicates and, if we allow it to, illuminates.

In a similar manner, creative activity for the artist is a dream that does not provide for a "working through" of a basic conflict but is merely a statement, in artistic language. The artist does not "solve" his fundamental problems with the artistic creation anymore than we "solve" our problems by producing a dream. The *information* is available for interpreting. This, however, is not the task of the artist or the *raison d'etre* for the oeuvre.

There is a continuing presence of neurotic themes throughout any artists' work; and artistic creativity, by itself, does not provide solutions to unconscious conflicts. Such "solutions" can only have temporary therapeutic value for the artist. Anna Freud once said, *"Even the highly prized and universally envied gift of creative activity may fail tragically to provide sufficient outlets or acceptable solutions for the relief of intolerable internal conflicts and overwhelming destructive powers active within the personality."*

Such was the situation with Van Gogh. We can more easily explain, however, his intrapsychic conflicts than grasp what it was that enabled this artist to paint at all. Psychoanalysts such as Ernst Kris and Phyllis Greenacre have discussed and shared these views and also marveled at the mystery of artistic creation, seemingly unexplainable by any technique. Van Gogh's paintings, with all of their originality and passion, continue to live more than 100 years after they were created.

Van Gogh produced more than 1600 works of art, approximately 840 of which were paintings done within the last two years of his life. His productive artistic span lasted approximately ten years. His most representative works were all created in two and a half years—a time when he had moved to Arles and was hospitalized much of the time. It was then that he began to express violent feelings—many of which were related unconsciously to his father, but (by the processes of *condensation and displacement as in the dream*) were depicted in the representation of landscape, flowers and the human face. Later they became directly related to his friend and fellow artist Gauguin. Importantly, Van Gogh used natural objects as *representations of his inner state of mind.* He painted what he *felt* as much as what he saw and had a unique way of seeing. The world filtered through his own conflicts. We *all* see the world filtered through *our own* conflicts and experiences, and we resonate with the artist who speaks to our unconscious. Van Gogh represented nature in his own way—an (unconscious) idiosyncratic interpretation of nature. Some of the colors he used in depicting natural objects, such as stars and flowers, have, one hundred years later, been confirmed by scientists using high resolution telescopes and other sophisticated equipment.

Van Gogh rendered the full intensity of his emotions creatively and painted expressions of his feelings and, as he once explained to his brother Theo, his intention was to paint *misrepresentations.* In so doing, he anticipated presenting the world with a greater reality than existed in the two-dimensional sense and in the visual sphere as well.

Van Gogh painted with the simplest and most personal means—he painted what he *felt* and knew through his unconscious. He used the best pigments and materials. The forms are clearly outlined, color is emphasized to the limit, and three dimensional viewing is essentially played down. His canvases are extremist in nature and have a hallucinatory quality. In his last works he used sparrows and wavy brush strokes, perhaps to convey the storms raging within him. His "madness" stimulated his artistic gifts.

Some psychoanalytic authors discuss his artistic work as a substitute for sexual behavior, including masturbation. This is highly theoretical and not as simplistic as it sounds. It refers to the "passage" of sexualized energy (libido) through various stages with the "end point" resulting in a specific activity. We do know that Van Gogh regarded the presentation of his art work as the production of babies for and with his brother, Theo. There is a great deal of psychoanalytic evidence for this interpretation, as well as Van Gogh's own statements in letters to his brother. Once again, we find the transition from (unconscious) fantasy to reality. From wish to creation.

Van Gogh was influenced by the Impressionists, having been introduced to them by Theo, and encouraged to pursue work with them. He transformed the Impressionist brush stroke into patterns of vibrant, jagged forms. His portraits have intense color sometimes applied straight from the tube! His draftsmanship combined with the color constitutes one of the most intensely expressive artistic achievements of the late nineteenth century and certainly the most personal. In fact, it would appear that Van Gogh took up where Rembrandt and Vermer had left off. Van Gogh, Gauguin and Cezanne brought to fruition the full implications of the Impressionist breakthrough and translated them *expressively.*

Van Gogh demonstrated how colors can be used to achieve intensely expressive *affects* and we find that he has revealed an "inner ecstatic vision." His visual potential for the use of color and light was technically activated by Impressionism. Even Pablo Picasso looked upon Van Gogh as the standard against whom he was destined to measure himself. Picasso and Van Gogh were men of the same generation who arrived in Paris only fifteen years apart. Picasso considered Van Gogh as living in accord with the highest artistic ideas.

While art historians and writers focus on Vincent Van Gogh's relationship (and especially correspondence) with Theo, many neglect and don't understand the most important relationship of his life: the *sibling relationship* that shaped his psychodynamics—his personality, his life and his fate. We tend to overlook or minimize what we don't understand or, perhaps, are afraid to understand. We do not wish to believe that events of childhood that seem so neglectful of significance can be of major importance in the shaping of our lives. This is natural because it is uncomfortable and anxiety-provoking to face and grapple with forces and events we do not understand and can't control. In such situations we ignore what is before us, dismissing events as irrelevant. Or, we mystify events and attribute them to a supernatural control.

Psychoanalysis has helped shed light on early childhood events and their impact on our lives—even events that have had an interpersonal significance before our birth, We must, however, have the courage to face that significance.

Vincent Willhem Van Gogh was born in 1852 and was stillborn. Exactly the same day of the same month a year later a second child was born and also named Vincent Willhem Van Gogh. This second child came into the world without an identity of his own; he was a *substitute* for his dead brother. In fact, his brother was buried near the entrance to his father's chapel and the living child frequently saw his own name on a gravestone; perhaps he saw it daily. Early on he acquired a conviction of his own inadequacy and vulnerability, had problems with regard to abandonment, separation and attachment, and developed a close symbiotic relationship with Theo, without whom he would have been unable to paint. In a sense, he could assume an identity and legitimacy only through Theo. Theo gave him the "license" to be productive and Vincent, himself, referred to his paintings as "their babies."

Van Gogh spent his life struggling with ambivalent feelings toward father figures. He had to deal with strong unconscious, homosexual longings directed towards Theo as well as to other artists such as Gauguin. Van Gogh suffered from a variety of physical problems associated with the excessive use of Absinthe; the use of camphor, which he placed under his pillow to induce sleep; the ingestion of pigments, turpentine and kerosene while painting both as a habit as an intentional suicide gesture; excessive use of bromides for sleep; excessive use of alcohol; the possibility of epilepsy and of central nervous system damage in association with syphilis or midbrain damage which resulted in direct sleep disturbance or Meniere's syndrome. Meniere's syndrome is a noninfectious complex neurological disturbance involving the inner ear. It produces disturbances in equilibrium resulting in dizziness or vertigo. Midbrain damage, also noninfectious, is not necessarily related to Meniere's syndrome but it can produce sleep disturbances because of the sleep "centers" that regulate somnolence and wakefulness.

Van Gogh's illness, however, was a process of mental instability following a long line of developmental and historical turns throughout his life and *related to specific psychological events of an internal and external nature.* As a result of deep-rooted guilt feelings, most of which may have resulted from the *substitute child syndrome* (the loss of his brother and his replacing him in life) and unconscious feelings he may have internalized from his relationship with his parents, especially his mother. Such feelings remain hidden and repressed from consciousness with outward manifestations only in the form of aberrant behavior. Such individuals tend to thwart success and move from points of near-success only to start over at another task and give up the ones they are working on. (A recent highly successful author, John Paul Evans, wrote *The Christmas Box* and has described how his deceased sister, whom he never knew and whose name could not be spoken in the household, influenced his decision to write a book with a very specific theme— that of a deceased child. When he told his mother the source of his inspiration, she cried).

Other manifestations of this repressed guilt include a tendency to damage the body by excess. Ultimately, Van Gogh could not accept the favorable reviews being written about him and the fame that was becoming obvious. At this point he committed suicide.

Van Gogh painted over forty self-portraits which may be seen as repeated efforts to understand and explore himself. The artist attempting to "work through" his conflicts and inner demons. These attempts at *self-definition* were to bolster a fragmented sense of self. The infant delights in the first moment of recognition of its own image in a mirror and ultimately the child sees itself mirrored in the mother's eyes. Artists use self-portraits to objectify themselves—although from the artist's own subjective perspective. As psychoanalyst W.W. Meissner noted, the self-portrait then becomes a "metaphor of the mind."

The *psychoanalyst*, Humberto Nagera, analyzed several of Van Gogh's paintings, especially the pictures representing two chairs. In

1888, Van Gogh painted two pictures representing an *empty* chair. The empty chair, known as *Vincent's Chair* or *The Yellow Chair*, is in the Tate Gallery in London. *Gauguin's Chair* is in a private collection. The first, *Vincent's Chair*, is very simple, primitive and rustic. His signature appears on a box in the corner. The chair is expressive, possibly because of the conscious use of light. There is an integrated harmony of color with the unpainted chair being yellow and the use of red surrounding it. Van Gogh's respect for the familiar, a chair in this case, is said by some to be so profound as to transform these objects into living beings. This relates to the transitional object phenomenon and the ability of the artist to "play" until there is a connection—an artistic creation—from internal reality to external life. We owe Dr. Nagera for our understanding of the inner dynamics of Van Gogh's mind and the understanding that the chair possibly represents a symbol of stability in Van Gogh's world of continued crises and the unconscious significance of the chairs.

On Vincent's chair we find his pipe and tobacco. However, Gauguin's chair is totally different; much more refined and feminine. Anticipating the arrival of his friend and fellow artist Gauguin, Van Gogh prepared a room much as an individual might prepare for the visit of his mistress. The chair would fit into a beautiful boudoir and is appropriate for the room Van Gogh prepared for Gauguin. Psychoanalyst Harold Blum noted, "Van Gogh was homoerotically attracted to Gauguin and transferred to him the desire to be reunited with the powerful father.

The background in *Gauguin's Chair* is very different from the first chair painting. There is a carpet on the floor instead of rustic tiles. The wall is a deep green color and there is a light. On the chair is a candle burning and by its side are novels, modern according to Van

Gogh's own description. Authors have noted that Gauguin's chair represents a night scene reflecting his personal style as well as its influence on Van Gogh.

Vincent Van Gogh had actually purchased Gauguin's chair before the latter arrived in Arles. We know that Gauguin was both a powerful father figure for Van Gogh and a substitute for the symbiotic relationship Van Gogh had with Theo. He may have also been a "replacement figure" for the unconscious feelings Van Gogh harbored towards his dead brother. This becomes all the more understandable when one examines the intensity of his bisexual conflicts and his unconscious, passive feminine longings. No doubt these feelings were stirred up by Gauguin's impending visit.

Gauguin was also attempting to deal with his underlying passive, feminine longings as the result of being a fatherless child— something that may account for his "supermasculine" behavior. According to psychoanalysts and Dr. Nagera, Van Gogh's defense against his feelings was, in his *unconscious mind*, to turn Gauguin into a woman. He also expected Gauguin to take a feminine role in the household by, for example, doing the cooking. Van Gogh could not be a follower, yet Gauguin was expecting to be the leader and this resulted in the clash that occurred later. When Gauguin finally arrived on October 20, 1888, Van Gogh was revived in spirits and enthusiasm. Gauguin took charge, however. He organized the routine of the household and asserted his authoritarian and arrogant personality. It was only a matter of time before Van Gogh became resentful.

Gauguin continued to be "successful" with women. Van Gogh was not, and his own potency at this time was already failing, possibly as a result of the changes in physiology of a toxic nature. Van Gogh was, in a sense, poisoning himself and we find here an interplay of the physical and the psychological. This was no mind-body dichotomy, but an integration of pathology.

Van Gogh knew Gauguin wanted to leave Arles but the idea of his going away and abandoning Van Gogh resonated with earlier themes of abandonment (psychological and "real") and resulted in further conflict. For Van Gogh, this was the ultimate catastrophe. As W.W. Meissner notes, Van Gogh's self-portrait from late 1888 reveals "the face is bony, angular; the eyes once more sullen, piercing and accusing. There is nothing friendly or accommodating about it. It *is a face that is stretched tautly over an inner force that seems held in check only by considerable effort* (emphasis added.)" These conflicts led Van Gogh to attempt to mutilate Gauguin with a razor, an act which concluded in Van Gogh's infamous self-mutilation by cutting off his ear lobe. As Humberto Nagera described, Van Gogh painted his own empty chair and Gauguin's empty chair just before Christmas, which was before he attacked Gauguin with the razor. He thus unconsciously passed the death sentence on them both, represented by *the empty chairs*.

According to Dr. Nagera, "The pipe and tobacco pouch on Van Gogh's chair are genital symbols." These objects are located in the position that would be occupied by the genitals if individuals were sitting in the chairs. Nagera notes that Van Gogh's representation is impotence and infertility contrasted with Gauguin's candle, large, erect and glowing. Gauguin's "phallus" stands next to two artistic creations (books). Gauguin's arm chair alone is more phallic than Van Gogh's simple chair—it emphasizes an additional appendage. This is a psychoanalytic interpretation based on clinical experience, biography and theory. Psychoanalyst Harold Blum wrote, "Van Gogh's chair paintings, reminiscent of father and his paternal sexuality, are painted with an ardor appropriate to the awesome feelings invested in them.

The empty chairs as death symbols for Van Gogh is confirmed in the letters he wrote to Theo. In psychoanalysis, a patient *free associates*—that is, the patient talks about anything in his or her mind. When we examine diaries, letters or other communications of writers and artists we treat this material as "free associative" and make interpretations based on past experience and theoretical constructs. Van Gogh's "associations" refer to the symbolic representation of death based on a drawing of the empty chair by the artist. This is not a magic or mystical interpretation but is based on material produced by the Van Gogh as the artist-patient.

Van Gogh wrote, "Empty chairs—there are many more of them, there will be even more, and sooner or later there will be nothing but empty chairs..." The *conscious* link with death is quite clear. Importantly, this likely refers to the empty chair at home—*that of his dead brother.* There is a continuing sense of guilt for the death of the last sibling.

In a similar fashion, Van Gogh responds to one of Theo's letters during the Amsterdam period after his father left. Van Gogh went to his room and looked at the table in which the books and the copy books of the day were set forward. There was the empty chair where his father had been sitting. Van Gogh behaved as if his father had died or was about to die; musing that perhaps he would never see his father again. W.W. Meissner writes, "There was within him a hidden enemy, a persecutor and exterminator who had the power to destroy him."

Psychoanalysis has taught us that we love our enemies and hate even our friends and family. Relationships are ambivalent. Van Gogh's father's departure may have reactivated the hostility and death wishes aroused by being left at school away from home many years earlier. This in turn relates to Gauguin by the process of *transference*. Although transference, strictly speaking, is a transfer of feelings from earlier important relationships to the therapist and occurs only (in pure form) in a treatment situation, we do "transfer" feelings from the past to important "transference figures" in our adult life, outside formal therapeutic settings. Dr. Nagera explains how the particular books of Van Gogh's father appear as an element on Gauguin's empty chair by the side of the burning candle. The candle, itself, being not only a sign of Gauguin's virility in contrast to Van Gogh's impotency, but also of Gauguin's death as well as that of the father.

Van Gogh's reaction to Gauguin's impending departure from Arles can be understood because his attacks on Gauguin were a manifestation in actual behavior of his hostilities and death wishes against his father. The situation was re-enforced by the hostility towards Theo and Gauguin himself. Gauguin had became a *transference figure.* Van Gogh's defiant and aggressive behavior may be seen as a defensive maneuver to cope with his underlying feelings of insecurity and 'identity diffusion.'"

After Vincent Van Gogh's father's death, Van Gogh painted a commemorative picture, a blue vase with flowers on the table. Dr. Nagera explored this work as well. By the side of the vase lie the father's pipe and tobacco pouch. This is the first time that the pipe and tobacco pouch symbolism appeared in Van Gogh's paintings. Harold Blum noted "The figures in the chairs are blocked out except for the *genitals* which became most prominent, *though symbolically disguised"* (emphasis added).

In Vincent's own empty chair, we can recognize the two elements of the pipe and tobacco lying on the chair as representing, in symbolic terms, his father's death. In the vase painting those items are now Van Gogh's *own* pipe and tobacco lying on the chair. They are an indication of his *own death* through "the Tallyon law" of the unconscious. These objects point to the symbolic crimes he has committed: his death wish towards his father and the death of a sibling—one year before his birth. Apparently, Van Gogh had been living with a ghost.

In the painting *Vase of Flowers*, the flowers mourn the father's castration and death simultaneously. This is a difficult interpretation for many to accept but there is a theme of the sower fertilizing the earth—the father making the earth flower. (In Van Gogh's mind, Dickens was also a symbol of the creative father. The symbols of seed, genitalia, offspring, flowers and the concept of immortality go hand-in-hand).

The empty chair signified the "fulfillment of the death wish towards the father figure, but it also served as a monument for his own preservation," according to Dr. Nagera, who also wrote "Van Gogh's execution of his own empty chair was symbolic of his hostile identification with father and his acceptance of the supreme penalty for this hostility." We unconsciously know what we deserve. The inner relatedness of these symbols is apparent as Van Gogh simultaneously paints his father—Gauguin's chair—and his own. Van Gogh's attack on Gauguin represented a re-enactment of the conflict of his hostility towards his father and the repressed feelings about his father's death. Van Gogh has, in symbolic terms, committed the Oedipal crime and must die. And, he did so, not long after this incident. The deep sadness and alienation is expressed in his self-portraits as well, especially in his eyes.

We find a similar theme in *Hamlet*. These theoretical constructs and explanations have a basis in reality and are manifested by specific behaviors. In Van Gogh's case, this was manifested by his suicide. The earlobe amputation is symbolic of the castration which included surrendering to a prostitute. In a sense, Van Gogh imposed upon himself a punishment he thought his father had ready for him when he rebelled against authority. Significantly, he had rushed bleeding to the Bout d'Arles and offered the severed lobe to one of the prostitutes there. A final (symbolized) surrender.

The punishment was confinement in the mental institution at St. Remy where Van Gogh was admitted. We must keep in mind that Van Gogh's, and anyone's, thought processes in this circumstance is not necessarily conscious. Blum noted, "In painting the chairs, Van Gogh compared his weak sexuality to his virile, omnipotent father-substitute, murdered and mourned the castrating father, revered the paternal penis, and sublimated his longed-for union with father and father's phallus."

Dr. Nagera also tells us that from the time Van Gogh cut his ear-lobe off, there was a significant change in his signature indicating symbolic castration (another unconscious equivalent of death). The "V," which was previously quite sharp, took on a rounded form, all the sharpness disappeared. The rounded letter became a permanent feature of his signature from this point on.

After the events surrounding his conflicts with Gauguin and his self-mutilation, he painted two self-portraits showing himself with the bandaged ear. As Meissner noted, "The face seems to bear an expression of desperation and self-absorption. It is a face that has borne the burdens of life too long—we would not be surprised were it to burst into tears."

Psychoanalyst H.R. Groetz noted, "Whenever Vincent painted a self-portrait, it was in order to place before his own eyes, and thus to make more objective, his search into himself."

Thus, in examining Van Gogh's work using the familiar mental processes of *dream analysis, condensation* and *multiple determination*, we discover one of the reasons for the dramatic impact of the paintings of the empty chairs. *Multiple determination* is a concept that was developed by one of my teachers, the psychoanalyst Robert Waelder.

It involves an understanding that many issues and symbols condense to focus on a particular constellation of behaviors or conflicts. In this sense, Van Gogh's death is multi-determined. No doubt it was influenced in part by a response to his brother's serious illness and in part to his own unconscious "pressure" pertaining to his fantasies (conscious and unconscious) regarding the death of his father, Gauguin, his nephew and, importantly, his brother Willhem. In his own *unconscious* Van Gogh had killed them all. This last self-portrait completed in September 1889, was for his mother in an attempt to reassure her that he was sane and well, yet the eyes are *sad* and reflect loss and despair. This disturbing image depicts the inner reality of the artist.

Related to all of this is a major external factor. His suicidal despair in the spring of 1890 resulted in his inability to accept greatness just at a point when his greatness was being recognized. (In practice we often find that "successful" individuals destroy themselves with drugs, suicide or "toxic relationships" at the point of success. Their unconscious does not allow the success). With Van Gogh, he could not acknowledge the ultimate significance of his work as "the greatest statement of his people since that of Rembrandt." In other words, he could no longer continue to maintain that he was no better an artist than his predecessors. To succeed was to be dead like his brother before him.

Two Chairs And A Vase: Symbolism in the Art of Van Gogh
Contributing Factors to Van Gogh's Illness

Consumption of Absinthe which was likely quite poisonous.
Use of camphor which Van Gogh placed under his pillow in order to sleep.

Ingestion of pigments, turpentine, and kerosene while painting, both as a habit and as an intentional suicide gesture.

Self-treatment with bromides for sleep.

Excessive use of alcohol.

The possibility of syphilis.

The possibility of CNS damage associated with midbrain damage, resulting in a sleep disturbance.

The possibility of Meniere's disease.

The possibility of epilepsy, either psychogenic or grand mal.

The likely possibility of manic depressive illness (bipolar psychosis).

The possibility of schizophrenia or schizophreniform psychosis.

Very significant psychodynamic issues associated with the replacement child syndrome and psychosexual conflicts and identification problems. These were major issues throughout Van Gogh's life.

Chronic sunstroke—based on his exposure while painting in Southern France.

Menigo-encephalitis—possibly associated with syphilis or other infections.

Christmas depression (see Christmas chronology.)

Several Major Catastrophes in Van Gogh's Life
Occurring at Christmas

Christmas 1874—Van Gogh is extremely despondent regarding Ursula's rejection.

Christmas 1875—Van Gogh leaves Goupils to go home, without notice, at their busiest time.

Christmas 1876—Van Gogh's father calls him back from England where he failed to hold down two jobs.

8. LIVING WITH A GHOST—VINCENT VAN GOGH

Christmas 1877—Van Gogh is a theological student in Amsterdam; he is miserable.

Christmas 1878—Van Gogh is a struggling evangelist at the Borinage.

Christmas 1879—Van Gogh is a vagabond, estranged from his family.

Christmas 1880—Van Gogh is an art student in Brussels. He ignored the holiday.

Christmas 1881—Van Gogh leaves his Etten home on Christmas Day after a violent quarrel with his father.

Christmas 1882—Van Gogh is in The Hague with a prostitute. He had just quarreled with his friend, Mauve.

Christmas 1883—Van Gogh returns to his parent's home at Nuenen because he fears having a nervous breakdown.

Christmas 1884—Van Gogh spends the day with his parents in Nuenen. He commented, "I was never more gloomy."

Christmas 1885—Van Gogh wanders around the outskirts of Antwerp in despair. He thinks about returning to the Borinage.

Christmas 1886—Unrecorded.

Christmas 1887—Van Gogh has a crisis: confusion and a psychotic episode at St. Remy.

Christmas 1888—Van Gogh is at Arles; he cuts off his ear.

Christmas 1889—Van Gogh is at St. Remy. He anticipated, and experienced, his longest attack.

It is interesting to note elements of a seasonal periodicity in Van Gogh's illness as this sometimes occurs in manic depressive psychosis.

9

THE MAN WHO STARTLED HIS CONTEMPORARIES: LEONARDO da VINCI

"Many, perhaps most, people are locked inside a safe. Their dreams, aspirations and even love become inaccessible. These valued jewels of a forgotten past are hidden. However, there are a few people who remain free and fortunate enough to partake of the sublimity of life."

— Ronald Turco

In 1994, computer scientist Bill Gates paid the estate of Armand Hammer $30.8 million for 18 sheets of linen paper folded in half. This is a notebook Leonardo da Vinci composed between 1508 and 1510 known as the *Codex Leichester*. Although it contains little of Leonardo's spectacular drawings and draftsmanship, it does demonstrate his enormous powers as a modern scientific thinker. He was clearly a man ahead of his time.

Leonardo was born in 1452 in the little town of Vinci between Florence and Empoli. He was the illegitimate child who joined his father's household at the age of five, having previously resided with his "poor forsaken" mother. The year Leonardo was born, his father married the sixteen-year-old Albiera Amadora, who remained childless and died twelve years later. Leonardo's mother married a man nicknamed Accattabriga—the Quarreler. Leonardo thus had unmarried parents, a stepmother, stepfather, several half-sisters and a half-brother. There is evidence that, in 1457, he was living with his grandparents at least for a brief time. He continued, however, to have a close relationship with his mother.

Leonardo had a private, "quiet" childhood and grew up to be a gentle and kind man. Even while learning art as a young person, Leonardo was fascinated by everything. He devoted his time to study the various sciences, "The desire to know is natural to good men." He wanted to possess all forms of knowledge especially applicable to his art. This child, raised by two mothers, was stimulated to create and *project* in artistic creation. When he looked into the darkness of a large cave he wanted to see "...if it contained some miraculous thing." He had a reverence for all living creatures, was fascinated by everything.

Perhaps the best adjective to describe Leonardo da Vinci would be *enigmatic*. Even a century after his death, the only evidence of his work and philosophy was hidden away in private collections. He worked painstakingly, but interestingly, was ambivalent about both his scientific and artistic work, and procrastinated so long that he often failed to complete the goals and tasks he set for himself. His procrastination became part of his reputation and he set a record for time elapsed between accepting a commission and delivering the finished painting— twenty-three years!!

Leonardo was also something of a "dandy" and in later years was described as "the master with the white beard." He was eccentric and could be intimidating. Some felt Leonardo was supernatural. Some considered him a magician or a fantastic creature—a sorcerer. Some thought of him as not of this world. Leonardo would probably fit the contemporary view of a clandestine agent—a spy. He was a solitary genius with a penchant for secrecy. He both wrote and decoded cryptograms. He tried to decipher occult messages from the past. He was ambidextrous and could write with equal ease forward and backward with inverted characters (mirror writing) to help conceal his studies. Perhaps the equality of his hemispheres (non-dominance) allowed him to experience time and space differently. The secrecy helped increase the mystery surrounding him. He also dissected the bodies of dead criminals, sawed up their bones and then boasted of it—sometimes just to provoke.

According to the historian Vasari, Leonardo da Vinci was a man of "physical beauty beyond compare" and praised Leonardo's "terrible strength in argument, sustained by intelligence and memory." It is said he was so strong that with his right hand he could twist a horseshoe as if it were made of rubber.

Leonardo's unique, "venerable" silhouette was said to be famous in the streets of both Florence and Milan. His contemporaries never failed to comment on his physical description. His beard "combed and curled reached the middle of his chest…. He wore a rose colored garment, which reached only to the knee, although the fashion of the time was for longer clothes." Leonardo had such thick hair and beard and bushy eyebrows that he was described by Lomaxxo, a Melanese painter as "…the true model of the dignity of knowledge, like Hermes Trismegistus and Prometheus in antiquity." Others spoke of Leonardo's eccentricity—he was left-handed and a vegetarian. Certainly he was remembered wherever he went as "a man of learning." He was a legend in his own time, especially when considered in the context of his inventions and scientific pursuits.

On the other hand, Leonardo had a love for practical jokes. He once took a connecting tube attached the shriveled dried intestine of a bull to some bellows and placed the guts in one room while he stood with the bellows in another. When people arrived in the room he used the bellows and a huge balloon suddenly started to fill the room, crowding the people against the opposite wall!

In his early twenties Leonardo was involved in a scandal that changed his life. He was accused of sodomizing a 17-year-old apprentice goldsmith. The penalty could have been death. In Leonardo's time, there existed an institution that allowed anonymous denunciation to police concerned with the control of "vice." A box for these denunciations, called the "Tamburo," was posted outside the Palazzo Vecchio. On April 8, 1476 an accusation was made against five young Florentines, one of whom was Leonardo.

This episode resulted in Leonardo being summoned for interrogation and examination. The investigation lasted months but was eventually dropped—possibly as a result of private financial intervention. This entire affair was shrouded in secrecy but the charges were eventually dismissed and from that period on Leonardo lived less openly and even wrote that he would conduct his life "secretly, with only the darkness of the night for witness." The ordeal had a lasting impact on Leonardo and strengthened his inclination to suspicion so much so that it reached the point where he lost faith in men and viciously guarded his ideas for the rest of his life.

Leonardo was basically anticlerical although he believed in God. He discovered God in the beauty, natural order and harmony of nature. He referred to the creator as the inventor of everything. Painting, he describes, is "the granddaughter of nature and related to God." He sought to understand the Almighty by reflecting on His creations. Even in *The Last Supper,* he chose not to represent Jesus' presentation of the Eucharist, but instead depicted the moment when he tells his disciples one of them will betray him. This subject was close to his heart—purity confronted and opposed by men—as he likely did not believe that men were fundamentally good and humanity was likely rushing toward destruction. There are certainly elements of personal identification in his depiction of *The Last Supper.* In any event, Leonardo placed science and knowledge above religion and Christianity, although this aspect of him was suppressed during his lifetime to avoid scrutiny by the Inquisition.

He was also a very generous man and gave freely to others, especially to his friends. He was kind, "sweet" and eloquent. He was an accomplished musician and an outstanding teacher who changed the way we see the world. He loved creatures so much that when he passed places where birds were sold he would pay whatever was asked for them just so he could take them from their cages and let them fly off into the air. He gave them back their lost freedom—thereby expressing "real magnanimity."

As an adult he was quite cunning. He maneuvered around the royalties' engaging intrigues by sidestepping with apparent skill. He was adept at politics and could be as self-serving as he was generous. Always industrious, Leonardo worked hard and long hours even as a youth. His emphasis on work was to study objects from *nature, not imagination,* which was consistent with his avoidance of psychology. It's been said that he developed this skill to such an extent that he could see time in slow motion delaying its passage to observe the patterns of bird flight.

This intensely curious, enigmatic man encompassed all the qualities of a superior inventor, scientist and artist yet inhibited himself in fundamental ways that resulted in incomplete work. He was also psychologically defensive and only superficially insightful. For example, Leonardo had a vague idea that his interest in flight stemmed from his childhood fantasy of the bird but he never delved into this further and never showed an interest in learning about human psychology or behavior. We also find that Leonardo's urge for knowledge directed him to the external world, thus keeping him *away from* the investigation of the human mind. There were no experiments or writings on psychology.

Vasari described Leonardo as being "capricious and unstable" in connection with the unfinished paintings. He attempts a justification by stating, "His intelligence of art made him take on many projects but never finish any of them, since it seemed to him that the hand would never achieve the required perfection." Vasari states that Leonardo conceived of problems so subtle that he could never resolve them, despite his skill.

Whatever the inhibitions and incompletions in his work, Leonardo da Vinci made many contributions both in art and science. For example, he refined a feature of shadows hitherto overlooked by artists. This is called *sfumato*—the opposite of *chiaroscuro*. Leonardo noted that objects seen in the distance are not as sharp as those viewed close up. The crescent moon is an example. Distant objects are not seen as crisply as those nearer the eye and he suggested that artists work with this phenomenon to render landscapes more accurately. He also used variations on perspective to enhance the mystery of a painting. The *Mona Lisa* and *The Last Supper* are both examples of this. His *Proportions of the Human Figure*—the image of a nude man with outstretched arms—is symbolic of the Renaissance attitude of expressing the direct perspective of the artist. That is, making a bold statement with a unique point of view.

He was able to experience and communicate the subtleties of *depth* and *shade* like no other artist before him. His interest in geology, botany, hydraulic engineering and natural science may have been prompted by his early relationship to nature. He was one of the pioneers in the use of red chalk and his Turin self-portrait was done in this medium in 1512, when Leonardo was about sixty years old. It is perhaps one of his greatest masterpieces. His health was failing, his eyes were weakened and his teeth were gone. The portrait was done during a period of uncertainty in his life when he was also losing his patrons and had no one to turn to. This masterpiece is a search for himself—self-analysis. The portrait makes it difficult to envision Leonardo as the figure of striking beauty as he was known in his youth. The smooth, beardless face was covered with a white beard. Vasari said of Leonardo that he had such great presence that "one only had to see him for all sadness to vanish."

Modern science was born in the Renaissance and Leonardo was right in the middle of it. He described the principles of the camera. He interrupted time, urged young artists to work from nature, and wrote extensively on the science of mathematics and art, although he never published a book—only his prolific notes remain.

Leonardo believed that mathematics was the highest expression of the human mind. He invented the parachute, submarine, as well as scuba equipment and tank. His applications to science are substantial. His interest in movement brought him to studies of anatomy, both human and equine, and his drawings are both a delight and a wonder to behold. The science of anatomy influenced Renaissance art and Leonardo played a major role in this. In turn, the rise of science influenced him. As with the products of all creative behavior, Leonardo's art expressed many determinants including the *Zeitgeist* and the multiple unconscious processes operative from his early development. Certainly his behavior and work is to be understood as something well beyond external influences—a product of his unconscious and the abstraction and imaginative creativity of the artist. The artistic "solution' is a product of multiple functions.

Leonardo's "love affair with the world" may well have protected him from disappointments. This is the attitude established in early childhood—perhaps by the age of three—that allows the future creator the capacity to erect "collective alternatives." Leonardo wrote: *Quel maestro si drizza alla perfezione del arte, del quale l'opera e superata dal giudizi*— "Perfection in art is achieved by the master whose work is ruled by judgment."

Interestingly, Leonardo as a scientist was obsessed with specific ideas rooted partly in his unconscious fantasies and he searched the world for objects and opportunities to express them—although only in an investigatory and inventive fashion. The same pursuits are true of his paintings. There was a discipline underlying both activities.

Leonardo da Vinci was preoccupied with light throughout his life. He saw the eye as the "window of the soul, which embraced the beauty of the whole world... Who would believe that so small a space could contain all the images of the universe....?"

His interest in light served both his science and his paintings. His interest in images without things led him to be the first European artist to draw a landscape. This has been considered the symbolic step toward abstraction. He also encouraged imagination, anticipating later abstract artists.

Leonardo rarely mentioned his past in his notebooks. He kept notes of his observations, writing with a reverse left-handed script and writing only indirectly, if at all, about himself. He did not record his emotional experiences. He does not leave us much in terms of confidences. During the first thirty years of his life all we know about his career and itinerary are a few dates and a few questionable facts. It is in his notebook, the *Codex Atlanticus,* that one finds the major products of his mind, including the revelation, "The sun does not move."

Leonardo took on the caretaking of a young boy. Giacomo was a wayward, unpredictable child who behaved badly and caused Leonardo much trouble. Leonardo wrote about the experience in uncharacteristically open fashion in his notebook. There are no other instances where Leonardo wrote at such length about any human being. The youth cost him plenty and thus this situation offers an interesting insight into Leonardo's character.

Rather than discuss his feelings in his notebook, he wrote of the cost and objective external situations such as buying the boy clothes and keeping him out of trouble. Leonardo rescued this child from the street—from poverty. At least this is the most likely explanation of his arrival. He characterized Giacomo as "a thief," "liar," "obstinate," "greedy." The boy frequently stole from Leonardo and others, yet Leonardo tolerated and nurtured his presence. He does not mention scolding or punishing him. Leonardo was immensely fond of Giacomo and gave him presents, took him everywhere through Italy, and even remembered him in his will. The boy never improved and was christened *Salai*—"Limb of Satan" by Leonardo. The nickname stuck, and still Leonardo continued to spoil the boy and dress him in lavish clothes. Salai became a pupil, but *no ordinary pupil!* He had no talent for art and Leonardo had trouble even teaching the boy the rudiments of painting. A pupil without talent and an unreliable servant had "the face of an angel...ravishing grace and beauty." He forgave Salai the lies and thefts and made him look even more beautiful by dressing him in fine clothes. An angelic boy "with curly hair, light eyes and slightly sulky mouth" appears many times in Leonardo's drawings. The child was ten years old at the time of his arrival when he disturbed Leonardo's otherwise organized life. Even *twenty years later* one finds in Leonardo's notebooks continued examples of the stormy relationship with Salai. The amusement with which Leonardo observed this boy and his affection certainly leave open to question any darker motives he made have had in the relationship.

Leonardo's affects (emotional reactions) turned to the instinct for research and converted his *passion* into thirst for knowledge by applying himself to investigation with persistence and penetration—thus *substituting passion or love for full knowledge.*

Leonardo da Vinci's relationship and a confrontation with Michelangelo reveals much about his character. The two men strongly disliked each other. Leonardo dressed immaculately and wore the latest fashions. He often made snide and irreverent remarks about Michelangelo, describing him as having a coarse peasant-like appearance. Of course, Michelangelo, being a sculptor, was often covered with marble dust. Michelangelo in turn sneered and denigrated Leonardo's abilities, especially as a sculptor and considered him a dilettante. Following a verbal encounter in Florence, the two men never spoke to each other again. It is to Leonardo's credit, however, that he never wrote poorly of Michelangelo. Then again, personal statements about his losses and personal life are notably absent in his writings.

***

The art critic Kenneth Clark referred to Leonardo as "the Hamlet of art history" partly because of our ability to emotionally resonate with his work and partly as a result of the enigma of his life. Sigmund Freud attempted to explain the riddle—the enigma—of Leonardo: Who was he? Where did he come from? What did he do?

The subject of Leonardo da Vinci had already been raised as a major personality in Freud's letters to Fliess in October 1898. By 1907, Freud was reading a study of Leonardo and called it one of his favorite books. In October 1909, he wrote to Jung proclaiming, "The riddle of Leonardo da Vinci's character has suddenly become transparent to me." The same year he spoke to the Vienna Psychoanalytic Society on the subject. He used the term *pathography* for the psychoanalytic investigation of the relationship between an artist's life and his works and the interpretations based on these relationships.

This first model of pathography has come to be called *the fictive approach* by authors such as Ellen Handler Spitz. The second approach to evaluating art from a psychoanalytic approach uses Hartmann's concept of "conflict free," considered in the context of the "internal relations" of the work of art—autonomous in nature and combining the autonomous functions of the ego with the dynamic and structural aspects—with the result being a comprise. This has come to be known as the *documentary approach* and is characterized by R.S. Liebert in his psychoanalytic study of Michelangelo (see chapter 9 related reading at end of this book). The shift is from the presumed pathology of the artist to the body of his/her work. Although Freud has been criticized for not using a similar method, Robert Coles, a psychoanalyst, points out that by 1910 Freud was engaged in an in-depth inquiry of Leonardo and had read every book he could find. The third approach is thematic, characterized by psychoanalyst Martha Wolfenstein's studies, particularly in her examination of Rene Magritte. The *thematic approach* focuses on clinical material and psychic splitting—the maintenance of division between wish and knowledge.

By 1910 Freud had completed his study of Leonardo da Vinci, taking an interpretative context with emphasis on conflict and repetition and the analysis of drives and drive derivatives typical of classical Freudian theory.

Particularly important in the study of Leonardo da Vinci is to determine why he gradually abandoned his art work and turned intensely to scientific research, why he worked so slowly, and habitually left work unfinished, and what caused him to become more and more "introverted." The artist, in our studies, is in the position of being a patient but we do not have the opportunity to mine him directly, nor do we have the usual free-association material obtained through psychoanalysis. Nevertheless, the psychological findings operative in all of us govern both neurotic and normal activity and we attempt to extend the "tool" of analysis to the study of someone we have never met.

There are many examples of this, including studies of Woodrow Wilson, Adolph Hitler, Nikita Khruschev, Saddam Hussein and the recent development of "criminal" forensic profiling in search of the identities of serial killers and other homicide perpetrators. With profiles of any kind we try to use accumulated data from a variety of sources including contemporary biographies as well as our understanding of "psychic life." From the moment of birth there is a series of interconnected experiences which form the fabric of our mental life. Frequently these are associated with loss, and fears of loss. In discussing these mental issues we tend to ignore, at least for a time, the purely aesthetic aspects of works of art.

Freud's basic thesis is that Leonardo's problems—his incapacity for love whether heterosexual or homosexual, his indifference to artistic productions, his turning from the imaginative life of an artist to that of a scientist, his slowness in working and his inability to complete his paintings, can be traced to childhood experiences. Others have looked upon these problems as examples of his genius and I am convinced that resistances to a full understanding of this (for any artist) cannot be surmounted without a personal analysis. Art critics, authors and artists themselves, such as Georgia O'Keefe, are universally resistant to the application of psychoanalysis to artists and their works.

Leonardo's infantile wishes related to childhood sexual matters were sublimated or directed through his research. He substituted passion and love for knowledge. Freud wrote of Leonardo: "The stormy passions of a nature that inspires and consumes, passions in which other men have enjoyed their richest experience, appear not to have touched him." Thus, investigation took the place of acting and creating until "the connection with demands of his art were severed."

Freud's 1910 study of Leonardo da Vinci places great emphasis on one specific childhood memory. Leonardo had written that a vulture visited him in his cradle, opened Leonardo's mouth with its tail and began beating inside it. Freud posited that this act corresponded to the act of fellatio and served as a paradigm of Leonardo's passive homosexual wishes as well as his later curiosity about flight. Leonardo's wish to fly is understood as a longing for sexual performance (he later abruptly abandoned flight). Freud interpreted this memory fantasy as Leonardo's wish to return to the aggressive tenderness of his mother who provided erotic stimulation, emotional isolation and aggression as well as to his later manifested homosexuality. Freud further discusses the psychological mechanisms producing homosexuality.

Psychoanalytic studies of Leonardo do not often directly address the formal artistic and technical achievements of this genius. Although genius may never be "explained," we study the laws of the mind that govern creativity. In this regard, Freud has attempted to penetrate the illusion of art to a hidden and repressed truth, i.e., the early developmental experiences of the artist. We study *Hamlet* in the same manner. The artist is able to use his early experiences in the service of his art—the creative alternative—and in so doing is able to maintain the early affective responses or to somehow get in touch with them for creative work. In Leonardo's case, a memory precipitated by an adult experience recapitulated the childhood experience with the mother.

In the painting of *The Virgin and St. Anne,* the figures are similar to a *condensed* dream image. Dream mechanisms work in the same way by putting things together and sometimes fusing them and the result is the individual creative work—dream or work of art. We are more focused in this regard on the artist rather than the inherent nature of his production. We thus arrive at a point where we address the issue of Leonardo turning away from artistic creation to scientific researches and note the psychoanalytic perspective that "his infantile past had gained control over him."

In other words, Leonardo sublimated his erotic instinct. Initially he used science in the service of his art, learning about light, color, mechanical objects, form and anatomy but then he later assumed a "regressive shift" as he became impatient of painting and substituted scientific research in place of artistic creation. We know from clinical work that the first researches of childhood are concerned with the issues of sexuality, and Leonardo himself connected his urge for research and especially the study of flight to his vulture fantasy. He turned much attention to the study of the flight of birds.

Leonardo da Vinci cannot be said to love or hate, rather he distanced and removed himself from love or hatred. He investigated instead of loved. This is why his life was so much poorer in love than the lives of other artists. The original sexual instinctual forces directed to scientific—rather than artistic pursuits—resulted in a wave of sexual repression and compulsive research. Investigation took the place of acting and creating and although the research began in the service of his art with the desire to imitate nature, he was "swept away" until the demands of his art were severed. He discovered the general laws of mechanics, defined the stratification and fossilization in the Arno Valley and finally wrote: "*Il Sole Non Si Move*" (*"The Sun Does Not Move."*) His urge for knowledge of the external world kept him away from the investigation of the human mind. He approach was to become interested in a problem and behind the first problem, would find countless others. He had difficulty limiting his demands. Eventually, he would abandon his work of art as unfinished or declare that it was incomplete.

One wonders if Michelangelo's enmity toward Leonardo is associated with the awareness of this phenomenon. Psychoanalyst Ernst Kris agreed with Freud that Leonardo's obsessional scientific interest and defeating work habits related to infantile imprints but stated that we are yet unable to penetrate to the central problem of Leonardo's genius, noting "...this question remains unanswered." K.R. Eissler's hypothesis in regarding unresolved conflict stimulating creative work, and Phyllis Greenacre's theory of creative alternatives (described in chapter 1) must be considered in this context.

Other researchers, such as Dr. James Randall and Antonia Vallenti, dispute the homosexual implications of Leonardo's life. The relevance of sexual behavior to creativity, regardless of orientation, is not understood, and the issue is certainly not one of moral judgment but of scientific interest. There is no definite proof of that Leonardo engaged in homosexual behavior although the indications in his drawings and his relationships to attractive males supports Freud's view that it is "doubtful whether he ever embraced a woman with love." There is no record of a woman in Leonardo's adult life, however some maintain that he had no more sexual experience with men than with women. Leonardo appears to have felt revulsion to heterosexual relationships and condemned the "act of coupling." He warned against lustfulness. Freud stated, "He appears to us as a man whose sexual drives and activity were extraordinarily low, as if some higher aspiration lifted him above ordinary animal necessity."

Leonardo's instinctual forces were directed to investigation rather than artistic pursuits as he sublimated his libido into an urge for knowledge. In this regard, his "infantile past had gained control over him." Some of Leonardo's contemporaries did not look on his work as being "inhibited" and offered excuses for his failure to finish his work although it is clear he had self-defeating work habits. Some might even say that his scientific pursuits were synergistic with his artistic aims and the creativity of a genius may have been stimulated by unresolved conflict. Once again this brings us back to Phyllis Greenacre's hypothesis of creative *alternatives.*

Some of the most notable criticism of Freud's study involves his translation of the word "vulture." Freud's critics maintain that he mistranslated the Italian word *nibio,* which supposedly means kite. Freud attributed Leonardo's screen memory as a wish to return to the aggressive tenderness of his mother who provided the sensuality of his earliest experiences. He elaborated on the issue of fellatio by discussing the vulture-headed deity Mut, the Egyptian mother goddess, who is also represented with a phallus. Freud reasoned that Leonardo would have been familiar with these mythological details through study and exposure with the Church, which used the mythology to further the proposition of the virgin birth. If the word was mistranslated, the analogy with the Egyptian Goddess Mut would not be substantiated. This supposed error was noted in *Burlington Magazine* in 1923 and it is likely that members of Freud's inner circle were aware of this article and kept him up to date. Nevertheless, Freud held steadfast in his theory and maintained an interest in Leonardo at least until the 1920s, never wavering from his perspective of Leonardo's psychodynamics. In fact, in 1931 Freud maintained that *The Virgin and St. Anne* in the Louvre could not be understood without the specific childhood experience of the vulture.

Linguistic research into the word *nibio* supports Freud's translation and interpretation. Writers on the subject have simply repeated the initial criticism, thus perpetuating an incorrect assumption. Art historians I consulted are troubled by the psychoanalytic interpretation based on a single fantasy. Freud translated the Italian word *nibio* as *Geier*—vulture. In the *Dizionario Della Lingua Italiana*, the definition of *nibio* is "hawk; bird of prey." In fact there is a lengthy description (in Italian) of the bifurcated tail of this bird of prey, the velocity with which it swoops down upon its prey, and its aggressiveness. These descriptions substantiate Freud's understanding of Leonardo's screen memory and his affective responses to an aggressive (sexual) and sensuous mother. Going a step further, one notes that *Webster's Dictionary* (1975) defines *kite* as a hawk or a bird of prey and possibly a person who preys on others. *Kite* is defined as "any of certain birds of the hawk family with long narrow wings." One could argue that this is not sufficient support for an "unassailable" fact claim. We must then ask, How many dictionaries in how many languages should we consult?

Additional support for Freud's hypothesis is to be found in the writings of Leonardo himself. In the little notebook known as *Manuscript H,* Leonardo wrote, "It is said of the kite that when it sees its nestlings grow too fat, it pecks their sides out of envy and leaves them without food." Thus, in 1493, Leonardo spoke of kites as living creatures having "nestlings." He then goes on to discuss the female partridge being transformed into a male and forgetting its sex!

The linguistic issue has been diversionary. The significant criticisms are due to resistance. In fact, Freud had to deal with significant counter-transference issues when producing this study. He wanted to comprehend this "elusive-gifted" man even though he had access only to a limited amount of information, in a refined manner and with the limitations of the fictive approach to pathography even though he lacked an understanding of object relations and Leonard's self-psychology. In fact, Freud had not yet developed the structural model of the mind with the superego and ego represented in the unconscious (relegated only to the conscious in the topographical model).

Any artist has a tendency to substitute his own bodily experience and perceptions for that of the model he is working from. This "device" is used in many paintings. The artist is inclined to give figures he renders his own body experience and this is consistent with the psychoanalytic concept of the re-emergence of erotic experiences and childhood affects—feeling states. These early memories and feelings are stimulated by the creative process and by working with a model.

Freud noted, "We thus find a confirmation in another of Leonardo's works of our suspicion that the smile of Mona Lisa de Giocondo had awakened in him, as a grown man, the memory of the mother of his earliest childhood. From that time onward, Madonnas and aristocratic ladies were depicted in Italian painting humbly bowing their heads and smiling the strange, blissful smile of Catarena, the poor peasant girl who had brought into the world the splendid son who was destined to paint, to search and to suffer." Thus the Mona Lisa's smile has a double meaning: that of the promise of "unveiled tenderness" and the "sinister menace" from the early memory of the bird of prey. Thus, working from a model, Leonardo was stirred by the memory of his mothers' smile, and was restored, at least momentarily, to a state of infancy.

Freud also notes of Leonardo's mother, "So, like all unsatisfied mothers, she took her little son in place of her husband, and by the too early maturing of his eroticism robbed him of part of his masculinity. A mother's love for the infant she suckles and cares for is something far more profound than her later affection for the growing child…. When, in the prime of life, Leonardo once more encountered the smile of bliss and rapture which had once played on his mother's lips as she fondled him, he had long been under the dominance of an inhibition which forbade him ever again to desire such caresses from the lips of women." Freud observes that Leonardo went on to give all of his pictures— whether executed by himself or his pupils—the same blissful smile of the Mona Lisa.

The face of the Mona Lisa has been noted to resemble that of Leonardo himself. The resemblance is so close that he may have been painting himself or his mother, and Freud noted that it was "a perfect representation of the contrasts which dominate the erotic life of women; the contrast between reserve and seduction, and between the most devoted tenderness and a sensuality that is ruthlessly demanding— consuming men as if they were alien beings." The Mona Lisa has been called the womanly equivalent of Christ and the "consumer of all things."

Freud's studies of Moses, Michelangelo and Leonardo are highly personalized expressions of his evolving intellect and counter-transference mastery. Indeed, Freud himself was turning from the path of artistic fantasy to the logic of science and, in 1930, when he received the Goethe Prize for literature, noted that Goethe and not Leonardo had successfully blended the qualities of scientist and artist. This was at a time when Freud was being honored for his literary—not scientific— accomplishment. Freud's combination of personal experience, clinical observation, theoretical constructs and practical information has been called a "metaphor for the working of his mind."

Leonardo was a man capable of very strong emotions, especially of jealousy. Freud does not credit him enough with these emotions. A close study of Freud's interest in artists and their work reveals paradoxes, contrary opinions and, at times, attempts at "psychoanalysis" by a process of reductionism leaving the process of creativity un- explained—and clearly not given its due by the application of "sublimated sexuality." As Robert Coles noted in his article "On Psychohistory" published in *Psychohistory: Readings in the Method of Psychology, Psychoanalysis and History*, "The real question...is what Leonardo did with his life; not just with his neurosis...with his remarkable energy—his emerging intelligence, his perceptiveness, his sensitivity, his imagination...resourcefulness of spirit...artistic sensibility...(and) capacity to take note of how all sorts of things...including muscles and joints...work."

Freud, on the other hand, expressed an ambivalence of admir- ation and envy. Ernest Jones quoted Freud's reviews of the abilities of artists—two of whom he considered rivals for the affection of Martha, the woman who later became Freud's wife. "I think there is a general enmity between artists and those engaged in the details of scientific work. We know that they possess in their art a master key to open with ease all female hearts." This comment related partly to Freud's passionate attachment to Martha and his rivalry with Fritz Wahle, Martha's artist friend who Freud insisted was unconsciously in love with her. In a letter summing up his feelings about artists, Freud describes them as "people who have no occasion to submit their inner life to the strict control of reason." Is this not a contradiction in his criticism of Leonardo who investigated instead of loved?

This conflict in Freud's own personality evolved, and in its interference with an objective assessment of his subject we find the thread of his continuous preoccupation with himself and his identification with the characters of his work such as Oedipus, Hamlet, Leonardo and Goethe. In Freud's self-analysis, this pioneering achievement allowed him to grant a series of great men and characters with whom he identifies enough of their intrinsic qualities to convince us of his objective perception. Freud emerges at critical points in his pathographic presentations and even his most imposing work. *The Interpretation of Dreams* may be considered Freud's autobiography. Freud explored his Oedipal involvements, but only later, in the Leonardo da Vinci paper, was he able to assert that the highest and deepest satisfaction a man can have is as an infant suckling at his mother's breast.

I call your attention to Freud's "bird dream" in which he saw his beloved mother carried into a room by two people with birds' beaks. His mother was laid upon a bed. There is a similar consistency in the theme of "two mothers," as Freud also lost his surrogate mother—the Catholic nanny whom he believed to be the "originator" of his neurosis. This relates to his interpretation of *The Virgin and St. Anne.* The "two mothers" depicted may represent Leonardo's biological mother, Caterina (Saint Anne in the painting) from whom he was taken by his father, and his young stepmother (the Virgin). Thus, the artist has recapitulated his earlier developmental experiences by a creative process—a creative alternative. The "blissful smile" of the Mona Lisa is also seen on several androgynous figures represented in Leonardo's other paintings such as *Bacchus* and *St. John the Baptist.*

Freud also had to deal with a contest with his father and Wilhelm Fliess, his friend and correspondent. Freud discussed his ideas with Fliess, who in turn provided opinions. In reality, Fliess was probably a "stand-in" for Freud's father. This partial mastery became the substance of the subjective interpretation of Leonardo who had been abandoned by his own father, never to be fully accepted and loved. Freud's unconscious homosexual feelings toward Fliess, and his own father, and his underlying anxiety of them must also be considered in his perspective of Leonardo.

The homosexual wish of Leonardo is noted to be a defense against the sexual feelings for his mother, intensified by the absence of a male father figure, thus allowing Leonardo to remain erotically attached to his mother's image as a pre-Oedipal mother in a defensive-regressive position. We are therefore dealing with a highly eroticized internal object. Repressing this, putting himself in her place, identifying with her and taking his own person as a model from which to chose the objects of his love, was an indication of the manifestation of his homosexuality.

As Freud so succinctly stated, "...what he has in fact done was to slip back to autoerotism: for the boys whom he now loves as he grows up are after all only substituted figures and revivals of himself in childhood—boys whom he loves the way his mother loved him when he was a child. He finds the objects of his love along the path of narcissism. Psychological considerations of a deeper kind justify the assertion that a man who has become a homosexual in this way remains unconsciously fixated on the mnemonic image of his mother. By repressing his love for his mother, he perceives it in his unconscious and from now on remains faithful to her. While he seems to pursue boys and to be their lover, he is in reality running away from the other woman, who might cause him to be unfaithful...he hastens to transfer the excitation he has received from women on to a male object and in this manner repeats over and over again the mechanism by which he acquired his homosexuality." (Note that this is the first time Freud broached the subject of narcissism).

Freud may have been uneasy dealing with artists in and out of the consultation room. He may not have dealt with the aesthetic aspects of art as much as we would have liked. He did, however, penetrate the illusion of art looking to the hidden and repressed truth—the developmental experiences of the artist. As Jack Spector noted in *The Aesthetics of Freud: A Study in Psychoanalysis and Art,* "...he sought himself, but he did so with a constant awareness of an interest in the outer world, the objects (whether people or things) he contemplated being the other side of his interest in himself." Art—aesthetics—does not cure, but it does teach. Freud compared Leonardo to "a deep dark mirror." This man's activity in science, engineering, literature and art was dazzling yet he remains something of a secret. Leonardo wrote, "If you are alone you belong entirely to yourself. If you are accompanied by even one companion you belong only half to yourself, or even less."

Leonardo was perhaps the epitome of the "ideal man"—a philosopher, painter, and cultivated gentleman. Leonardo was depicted by Giovio, a man who had known him at the court of Pope Leo X, as a man of "charm and generosity" with a brilliant mind "not inferior to the beauty of the person.... His inventive genius was amazing, and he was the arbiter of all questions pertaining to beauty and elegance, in particular all those pertaining to ceremonial spectacle. He sang admirably, accompanying himself on the lira, and the entire court was delighted." Although solitary, Leonardo da Vinci remained generous, gentle, a witty conversationalist and musician to the end of his life. He died at the age of sixty-seven "to the great affliction of his friends."

10

THE END
IS THE
BEGINNING

"What we call the beginning
is often the end.
And to make our ends
is to make a beginning.
The end is where we start from."
— T.S. Eliot

Ernest Hemingway's mother wanted twins and raised her son as a girl; the companion of his older sister. He wore dresses, played with dolls and tea sets and learned to avoid intimacy. His preoccupation with masculinity is legendary. Leonardo da Vinci was infantalized and dominated by his mother to the extent that his view of women in his paintings, as well as his personal life, relates to their functioning as mothers. In discussing Leonardo's mother Sigmund Freud wrote, "Like all unsatisfied mothers, she took her little son in place of her husband, and by the too early maturing of his eroticism robbed him of a part of his masculinity." Yukio Mishima was infantalized by his grandmother;

Duke Ellington by his mother. All of these men avoided intimacy and developed defense mechanisms to deal with the underlying experiences and identification problems. The fathers in these circumstances became less than important—pushed aside. Ellington and Hemingway created idealized women who never met their expectations. Mishima and Leonardo developed identity problems of a different kind. Mishima was too close to feminine identity and overcompensated by bodily preoccupation. Leonardo was also too close, yet developed inhibitions in his work. Mishima emphasized creativity and the body. Leonardo turned to science and external sources of identity.

Mark Rothko never resolved the loss of his father and the incomplete identification that evolved from this relationship. He too had a strong, domineering mother. Vincent Van Gogh was a "replacement child" who produced his art—his "babies"—with and for his brother Theo, with whom he forged a exceptionally strong bond. Renee Magritte was replaced by the birth of two siblings when he was thirteen months old and, in early adolescence witnessed the naked body of his mother after she committed suicide by drowning. Edvard Munch experienced the loss of his mother and beloved older sister; his relationship with his father was problematic. Helen Hardin experienced loss through parental divorce and was devastated when she learned of her father's affair. Her relationship with her mother, also an artist, was complicated by rivalry and conflict beyond the usual mother-daughter squabbles. Her first marriage was abusive and problematic. The lives of these individuals also became complicated by celebrity status which interfered with their relationships and the possibility of reasonable outside intervention when their problems become insurmountable.

With Andrew Wyeth, we find a degree of normality not often encountered with artists. The stable, down-to-earth childhood, positive developmental experiences and good parenting allowed him the capacity to empathize with people and geography and to develop a stable long-term personal relationship with his wife Betsy. With Wyeth there is no mask.

Architecture is the science of designing and building *as if* the act were conscious. Looking behind the masks we find, even in the situation of psychological normality, that unconscious developmental experiences have a determining effect of the final product. Nevertheless, this does not "explain" creativity. This understanding does, however, help to explain the artist and the resultant art. Art is more than the acquisition of skills—it is the development of something new. A new way of representing themes—a new language. A personal evolution of discovery that goes well beyond logical thought and uses *primary process* thinking. This process bypasses logic and involves uncertainty and psychological risk-taking.

Creative people have the capacity to tolerate significant amounts of *ambiguity*. This is very important and especially noticeable in the work of Duke Ellington. The artistic product becomes the repository of the artist's unconscious projections whether we wish to call them healthy or unhealthy. The artist must set aside the ambiguous and paradoxical aspects of experience and allow play—the transitional experience—to dominate. Artwork then is simultaneously discovered and created, bridging the gap between the artist and the "outer world" of reality. In no other area of life do we find such a close alliance between the inner life of imagination and outer reality. The artist is able to tolerate the intensity of his inner experience and the anxiety that may go along with it as well. The product is new—not previously existing. What one has not seen before. The artist reconfigures external reality and draws on the developmental experiences to do so using an ability to associate these experiences with the artistic product. The creativity of the artist encompasses the ability to sustain ambiguity, to suspend logical thinking and allow imagination to dominate. The transitional experience becomes dominant. The artist re-experiences emotional issues dominant in childhood but frequently repressed. The ability to depict this material in universal terms with a poignant perspective becomes "palatable" to the observer. The universal unconscious problems are never solved through art but they are better understood and shared. The artist has allowed himself to *regress* in order to experience what most people simply repress. He is willing and able to experience the vulnerability associated with this process. To take a chance, so to speak. To use the creative alternatives in a passion to create.

Much has been said about mothers and relationship to mothers in this volume. Also significant in the lives of all individuals is the father. The father is the link for the child to the outside world. The father also helps the child, male or female, complete the sexual identity process. The father helps the developing child contain aggression and we find in the lives of some artists the dominance of the mother minimizing the father's significance with resultant psychopathology in the developing child. The father also enters into the picture regarding the developing motor phenomena of the child. The linking of early experience involving the body had been well noted by researchers such as Jean Piaget.

Freud described the ego as first and foremost a "body ego." The creative act moves to action—and the action is internal and external. The move is toward a less organized state of consciousness. The internal and external become ambiguous; consciousness is altered. The creative individual deals with this less structured "ego state" and earlier forms of experience become operative—the artist becomes what he is creating. This is the inspiration of his work. The artist's heightened sensory awareness occurs at all levels and has been (frequently without intent) fostered by developmental experiences and intense early relationships. Some artists speak of suspending consciousness entirely. For example, composer Richard Strauss once reported, "When in my most inspired moods, I have definite compelling visions involving a higher selfhood. I feel at such moments that I am tapping the source of Infinite and Eternal energy from which you and I and all things proceed...a Divine gift...a mandate from God." Richard Wagner reported, "My most beautiful melodies have come to me in dreams." Johannes Brahms wrote, "I am in a trance-like condition, hovering between being asleep and awake. I am still conscious, but right on the border of losing consciousness, and it is at such moments that inspired ideas come. All inspiration emanates from God and He can reveal Himself to us only through that spark of divinity within—through what modern psychologists call the subconscious mind."

These are interesting descriptions of the unconscious mental mechanisms at work and the "looseness" of pre-verbal material and ambiguity. The infantile experience of bliss can be characterized by Brahms' statement, "I felt that I was in tune with the Infinite and there is no thrill like it." Giacomo Puccini made similar statements about his creativity and the "supernatural influence" on his work.

The capacity to shift from unconscious to conscious material and what we psychiatrists call "shifting ego states" is characteristic of the creative individual. Creativity involves this ability to deal with primary and secondary process thinking and perhaps an added element of synthesis that creative artists possess. The creative person can call fourth earlier experiences and use them creatively. The creative person evolves a memory bouquet—a celebration of life. A mystery we love to pursue. A mystery we identify with—that adds pleasure and meaning to our life and one we hope will never end. A mystery that leads to ever greater depths of understanding and, like quantum physics, continues to open new avenues to understanding.

There is no scientific consensus on the nature of creativity. The creative impulse is a thing in itself; necessary for work in art and present in anyone looking at anything or doing something deliberately.

SUMMARY

Psychoanalysis offers a multidimensional approach to the study of art and artists by encompassing at least three overlapping points of view. The first is the *developmental perspective* which focuses on early childhood experience and especially parental (mother) interactions. This view deals with persistent themes in an individual's life—the "repetition compulsion." We repeat experiences—in reality or symbolically—in an attempt to master or "re-work" them. The resulting behavior becomes personality and character.

Psychoanalyst Phyllis Greenacre has made the most outstanding contributions to this area of study, especially in focusing on the artist's experience of being "special." She noted that gifted children have a more intense sensitivity to sensory stimulation and they "take in" more of their environment in an emotionally charged fashion calling this phenomenon "collective alternates"—the "love affair with the world."

William Niederland, another psychoanalyst, is also a proponent of the developmental approach and writes of the artist's attempt "at constant search for rebirth," including body-ego experiences. This concept resonates with our understanding of Yukio Mishima and his subjective experience and bodily preoccupation; a striving for completeness. D.W. Winnicott focused on the "good enough mothering" and the early maternal "holding" environment which allows the child (later artist) to be secure and free enough to play and create. Melanie Klein is another psychoanalytic theorist who focused on the developmental need to project to the mother and the world what was lacking "inside."

The second perspective focuses on the *conflicts* of an individual artist and his/her attempt to "compromise"—"multiple factor" in experience. Robert Waelder, one of the most dynamic and insightful psychoanalysts I have known, described this as the "principle of multiple function." The artist may be *sublimating* his conflicts as well, a perspective discussed by psychoanalyst Edmund Berger. The artist can then express what is "taboo" in the culture by producing socially acceptable art.

The third perspective encompasses *adaptation.* By creating, the artist can become complete with his internal and external environment. This is clearly illustrated in the life of Duke Ellington. There is an ongoing process of satisfaction. The artist becomes "comfortable" with what he is getting from the environment and is driven to continue the experience. These are the most psychologically healthy artists as they draw upon what has been described as the "conflict free" area of personality (ego). I like the term "regression in the service of the ego." Andrew Wyeth is another example of someone working from this perspective.

All of these perspectives overlap and are likely to be simultaneously operative in any artist's life. There are no rigid boundaries and all draw on "primary process material"—*the material from the unconscious and dreams later symbolized in the artistic production after condensation, displacement and reversal have occurred.* The themes persists throughout the artist's work. Psychoanalyst Ellen Handler Spitz noted: "No one who has ever been immersed in creative work in any medium of the arts—who has struggled and reveled in the world of the studio, felt its textures and muddle, its ambivalent persuasions, arrant abandonment of clock time, and the sudden elation as the gap closes between imagination and reality—could be persuaded to doubt the connections between such work, such moments, and the earliest of life's experiences."

SUGGESTED READINGS

1: Abstractions And Inner Reality

Bond, Alma H. *Who Killed Virginia Woolf? A Psychobiograhy.* Insight Books, Human Science Press, Inc. New York, 1989.

Bromberg, Norbert. "Hitler's Childhood." *International Review of Psychoanalysis*, 1974:227-244.

Clutterbuck, Richard Lewis. *Living With Terrorism*, Arlington House, London, 1976.

Fanteux, Kevin, Ph.D. "Beyond Unity: Religious Experience, Creativity and Psychology." *Journal of the American Academy of Psychoanalysis*, Vol. 23, No. 4. Winter, 1995:619-634.

Grolnick, Simon A. "Emily Dickinson: The Interweaving of Poetry and Personality." *Psychoanalytic Review,* Vol. 77, No. 1, Spring 1990:111-131.

Freud, Sigmund and Bullitt, William C. *Thomas Woodrow Wilson: A Psychological Study.* Houghton Mifflin Co., Boston, Mass., 1967.

Langer, Walter C. *The Mind of Adolph Hitler, The Secret Wartime Report.* Basic Books, Inc., New York, 1972.

Laswell, H.D. *Psychopathology and Politics.* Viking Press, New York, 1960.

Mahler, Margaret S., Pine, Fred, and Bergman, Anni. *The Psychological Birth of the Human Infant—Symbols and Individuation.* Basic Books, Inc., New York, 1975.

Podolsky, E. "The Last Murderer." *Medico-Legal Journal*, Vol. 33, 1965: 174-178.

Rank, Otto. *The Myth of the Birth of the Hero.* Alfred A. Knopf, New York, 1959.

Ressler, Robert K., Burgess, Ann W., Douglas, John E. *Sexual Homicide Patterns and Motives.* Lexington Books, D.C. Heath and Company, 1988

Rieder, Edmund G. "Unresolved Grief Reaction: Edvard Munch." *Psychiatric Annals*, 12:3, 1982.

Shaw, M. and Runco, M. (eds). *Creativity and Affect*. Ablex Publishing Corp., Norwood, New Jersey, 1994.

Spitz, Ellen Handler, *Museum of the Mind*. Yale University Press, New Haven, Conn., 1994.

——. *Art & Psyche: A Study in Psychoanalysis and Aesthetics*. Yale University Press, New Haven, Conn. & London, 1985.

Tuchman, Barbara W. "Can History Use Freud? The Case of Woodrow Wilson." *The Atlantic Monthly,* March 1967:39-44.

Turco, Ron. "Art and Psyche: A Study in Psychoanalysis and Aesthetics." *Journal of the American Academy of Psychoanalysis*, 21(3), 1993:465-475.

Wedge, Bryant. "Khruschev At a Distance: A Study of Public Personality. *Trans-Action*, Oct. 1968:24-28.

2: The Creation of Mood—Andrew Wyeth

Canady, John. *Mainstreams of Modern Art: David to Picasso*. Simon and Schuster, New York, 1959.

Fleming, William. *Arts and Ideas* (6th edition). Holt, Rinehart & Winston, New York & Chicago, 1980.

Hoving, Thomas. *Two Worlds of Andrew Wyeth: A Conversation with Andrew Wyeth*. Houghton Mifflin Co., Boston, 1978.

Hughes, Robert. *American Visions: The Epic History of Art in America*. Alfred A. Knopf, New York, 1997.

Novak, Barbara. *American Painting of the Nineteenth Century,* Icon Editions, Harper & Row, New York, 1969.

Strickler, Susan E., (ed.) *American Traditions in Watercolor; The Worcester Art Museum Collection*. Worcester Art Museum, Abbeville Press, New York, 1987.

Wilmerding, John. *Andrew Wyeth: The Helga Pictures*. Harry N. Abrams, Inc., New York, 1987.

Wyeth, Betsy James. *Christina's World*. Houghton Mifflin Co., Boston, 1982.

"Andrew Wyeth" An Exhibition organized by the Pennsylvania Academy of the Fine Arts, October/November 1966. Published by Abercrombie & Fitch Co., New York, 1966.

"The History of Art: From the French Revolution to the Present—Volume III." Random House, New York, 1981:226-227.

3: Reminiscing In Tempo—Duke Ellington

Apel, Willi & Daniel, Ralph T. *The Harvard Brief Dictionary of Music*. Washington Square Press, New York 1961.

Bellerby, Vic. *Duke Ellington: The Art of Jazz, Ragtime to Be-Bop*. Da Capo Press, New York, 1981:139-159.

Bennett, Lerone, Jr. *Before The Mayflower: A History of the Negro in America, 1619-1964.* Penguin Books, New York, 1966.

Bersani, Leo. *The Freudian Body: Psychoanalysis in Art.* Columbia University Press, New York:96-97 and 108-109.

Blesh, R. and Janis, H. *They All Played Ragtime: The True Story of an American Music*, Oak Publishing, New York, 1971.

Callahan, J. and Shashin J. *Models of Affect Response and Anorexia Nervosa.* New York Academy of Science, 1987, 504:214-259.

Campbell, Joseph with Bill Moyers. *The Power of Myth.* Doubleday, New York, London, Toronto, Sydney, Auckland, 1988, xix.

Collier, James L. *Duke Ellington.* Oxford University Press, Oxford, New York, Toronto, 1987.

Dance, Stanley. *The World of Duke Ellington.* Scribners, New York, 1970.

Ehrenzweig, A. *The Hidden Order of Art.* University of California Press, Berkeley, 1967.

Eissler, K.R. *Leonardo da Vinci: Psychoanalytic Notes on the Enigma.* International Universities Press, New York, 1967.

——. "Genius, Psychopathology and Creativity." *American Imago.* 1967, 24:35-81.

Ellington, Duke. *Music Is My Mistress.* Doubleday, Garden City, New York, 1973.

Ellington, Mercer with Dance, Stanley. *Duke Ellington in Person.* Houghton, Mifflin Co., Boston, 1978.

Erikson, E. *Young Man Luther: A Study in Psychoanalysis and History.* Norton, New York, 1958.

——. *Gandhi's Truth: On the Origins of Militant Nonviolence.* Norton, New York, 1963.

Fishburn, Hummel. *Fundamentals of Music Appreciation.* Longman's, Green & Co., New York, 1955.

Frosch, William A. "Moods, Madness and Music: Major Affective Disease and Musical Creativity." *Comprehensive Psychiatry,* 1987, 28:4:315-322.

Fox, Charles. "Duke Ellington in the Nineteen Thirties." *The Art of Jazz: Ragtime to Be-Bop.* Da Capo Press, Inc., New York, 1981, 123-138.

Freud, Sigmund. *The Complete Psychological Works of Sigmund Freud, Vol. XI.*, translated by James Strachey in collaboration with Anna Freud. The Hogarth Press and the Institute of Psychoanalysis, 1910.

——. *The Ego and the Id.* Standard Edition, Hogarth Press, London, 1923, 1957, 19:3-66.

Gammond, Petter. *Scott Joplin and the Ragtime Era.* St. Martin's Press, New York, 1975.

Gedo, John E. *Portraits of the Artist.* The Guilford Press, New York & London, 1983.

Greenacre, Phyllis. *Emotional Growth.* Two volumes. International Universities Press, New York, 1971.

——. "Woman as Artist." *Emotional Growth, Vol. 2,* International Universities Press, New York, 1960:575-591.

——. "Woman as Artist." *Emotional Growth.* International Universities Press, New York, 1971:448-529 and chapter 28.

——. "The Childhood of the Artist." *Emotional Growth, Vol. 2.* International Universities Press, New York, 1957, 1971:479-504.

Hasse, John Edward. *Beyond Category: The Life and Genius of Duke Ellington.* Simon & Schuster, New York, 1993.

Hooper, Joseph. "The Once and Future Duke." *Bazaar.* October 1993:106.

Jewell, Derek. *Duke: A Portrait of Duke Ellington.* Norton, New York, 1977.

Jones, Ernest. *The Life and Work of Sigmund Freud.* Edited by Lionel Trilling and Steven Marcus. Anchor Books, Doubleday & Company, Inc., Garden City, New York 1978.

Kohut, H. *Observations on the Psychological Functions of Music: The Search for the Self.* International Universities Press, New York, 1978, 233-253.

Kris, E. *Psychoanalytic Explorations in Art.* International Universities Press, New York, 1952.

Kris, E. and Kurz, Otto. *Legend, Myth and Magic in the Image of the Artist: An Historical Experiment.* Yale University Press, New Haven, 1934, 1979.

Lambert, G.E. *Duke Ellington.* Cassell, London, 1959.

Milner, M. *The Hands of the Living God: An Account of a Psychoanalytic Therapy.* International Universities Press, New York, 1969.

McDowad, M. "Transitional Tunes and Musical Development." *Psychoanalytic Study of the Child,* International Universities Press, 1970, 25:503-520.

Modell, Arnold H. *Object Love and Reality: An Introduction to a Psychoanalytic Theory of Object Relations.* International Universities Press, New York, 1968.

Nass, M. "On Hearing and Inspiration in the Composition of Music. *Psychoanalytic Quarterly,* 44:431-449.

——. "Some Considerations of a Psychoanalytic Interpretation of Music." *Psychoanalytic Quarterly.* 40:303-312.

Noy, P. "About Art and Artistic Talent." *International Journal of Psychoanalysis.* 1972, 53:243-249.

——. "Originality and Creativity." *So. Annual of Psychoanalysis,* 1984-85, 12-13:421-448.

Park, Edwards. "Around the Mall and Beyond." *Smithsonian.* December 1993:14-15.

Peck, Edwin. "Dylan Thomas: Verses of Music, Verses of Sorrow." *Annual of Psychoanalysis,* 1987, 15:293-309.

Roberts, John S. *Black Music of Two Worlds.* Praeger Publishers, Inc. New York, 1972.

Rose, G. "The Power of Form." *Psychological Issues, Monograph #44.* International Universities Press, New York, 1980.

Rose, Phyllis. "Jazz Cleopatra." Reprinted *Mirabella,* June 1989:230-243.

Rothenberg, A. "The Process of Janusian Thinking in Creativity," *Archives of General Psychiatry,* 1971, 24:195-205.

Seashore, Carl E. *Psychology of Music.* McGraw Hill Book Co., Inc., New York, 1938.

Schapiro, Meyer. "Leonardo and Freud: An Art-Historical Study." *Journal of the History of Ideas,* 1956, 17:147-178.

Sashin, J.I. "Duke Ellington's Life Seen as a Prime Example of Affect Tolerance." *The Psychiatric Times,* November 1988:35-36.

——. "Affect Tolerance: A Model of Affect Response Using Catastrophe

Theory." *Journal of Social Biol. Structure,* 1985, 8:175-202.

Sashin, J.I. and Callahan J. "Towards a Comprehensive Scientific Affect Theory." *American Psychoanalytic Assn., Scientific Meeting*, New York 1987.

Sidran, Ben. *Black Talk.* Da Capo Press, Inc. New York, 1971.

Sterba, R. "Toward the Problem of the Musical Process." *Psychoanalytic Review*, 1971, 33:37-43.

Turco, Ronald. "The Treatment of Unresolved Grief Following Loss of an Infant." *American Journal of Obstetrics and Gynecology,* 1981, 141:5:503-507.

Ulanov, Barry. *Duke Ellington.* Musicians Press, London, 1947.

Waelder, R. *Psychoanalytic Avenues to Art.* International Universities Press, New York, 1965.

———. "The Principle of Multiple Function." *Psychoanalytic Quarterly*, 1936, 5:45-62.

Ward, Geoffrey C. "Like His Music, The Duke Was Beyond Category." *Smithsonian*, May 1993: 62-74.

Waterman, Guy. "Ragtime." *The Art of Jazz.* Edited by Martin Williams, Da Capo Press, Inc., Plenium Publishing Corp., New York, 1980.

Winnicott, D.W. "The Location of Cultural Experience." *International Journal of Psychoanalysis*, 1967, 48:368-372.

Wittenberg, Rudoph. "Aspects of the Creative Process in Music: A Case Report." *So. Journal of the American Psychoanalytic Association,* 1980, 28:2:439-459.

4: The Object And The Dream—Mark Rothko

Ashton, Dore. *About Rothko.* Da Capo Press, New York, 1996.

Breslin, James E.B. *Mark Rothko: A Biography.* University of Chicago Press, Chicago & London, 1993.

Blesh, Rudi. *Modern Art USA: Men, Rebellion, Conquest—1900-1956*, Alfred A. Knopf, New York, 1956.

Clearwater, Bonnie. *Mark Rothko Works on Paper.* Hudson Hills Press, New York 1984.

Danto, Arthur C. *Encounters and Reflections: Art in the Historical Present.* Farrar Straus Giroux, New York 1986, 1990.

Fischer, John. "Mark Rothko: Portrait of the Artist as an Angry Man," *Harpers.* July 1970:16-23.

Goldwater, Robert. "Rothko's Black Paintings." *Art in America.* Vol. 59, No. 2, March/April 1971:58-63.

Hughes, Robert. *American Visions -The Epic History of Art in America.* Alfred A. Knopf, New York, 1997.

Novak, Barbara. *American Painting of the Nineteenth Century: Realism, Idealism, and the American Experience* (2nd edition). Harper & Row, New York 1969, 1979.

Shlain, Leonard. *Art & Physics: Parallel Visions in Space, Time & Light.* William Morrow & Company, Inc. New York, 1991.

The History of Art: The Random House Library of Painting and Sculpture

Volume 3.II "From the French Revolution to the Present." Random House, New York, 1981.

5: Mask And Steel: When Life Imitates Art—Yukio Mishima

Kitagawa. *On Understanding Japanese Religion.* Princeton University Press, Princeton, New Jersey, 1987.

Mishima, Yukio. *Ou la vision du vide.* Editions Gallimard, 1980.

——. *Confessions of a Mask (Kamen No Kokubaku).* New Directions Publishing Corp., New York, 1958.

——. *Forbidden Colors (Kinjiki).* Charles E. Tuttle, Co., Tokyo, Japan, Alfred A. Knopf, Inc., 1968.

——. *The Sailor Who Fell From Grace with the Sea (Gogo No Eiko).* Alfred A. Knopf, Inc., New York, Berkeley Medallion, 1965 and 1971.

——. *Patriotism.* New Directions, New York, 1966.

——. *Death In Midsummer (Manatsu Noshi).* New Directions, New York, 1966.

——. *Thirst For Love (Ai No Kawuki).* Perigee Book, G.P. Putnam, Alfred A. Knopf, Inc., New York, 1969.

——. *Spring Snow; Runaway Horses; The Temple of Dawn; The Decay of the Angel (Haru No Yuki)* (Tetralogy). Simon & Schuster, New York, 1968, Alfred A. Knopf, 1972.

——. *Sun and Steel.* Kodansha International, Tokyo, New York, 1982.

Nathan, John. *Mishima: A Biography.* Trousey, Tuttle Company, Suido 1-Chomey, 2-6, Bunkyo-Ku, Tokyo; Charles E. Tuttle, Co., Tokyo, 1974.

Rimer, J. Thomas. *A Reader's Guide to Japanese Literature.* Kodansha International, Tokyo and New York, *1988.*

Stokes, Henry Scott. *The Life and Death of Yukio Mishima.* Farrar, Straus and Giroux, New York, 1974.

Yamamoto, J. and Igo, M. "Japanese Suicide: Yasunari Kawabata and Yukio Mishima." *Journal of the American Academy of Psychoanalysis 3,* 1977:179-186.

Yourcenar, Marguerite. *Mishima: A Vision of the Void.* Translated from the French by Alberta Manguel. Farrar, Straus and Giroux, New York, 1986.

6: A Lion Among Women—Helen Hardin

Culley, LouAnn Faris. "Helen Hardin: A Retrospective." *American Indian Art Magazine,* September 1979:68-75.

Scott, Jay. *Changing Woman: The Life and Art of Helen Hardin.* Northland Publishing, Flagstaff, Ariz., 1989.

Shane, Karen. "Helen Hardin." *Southwest Art.* June 1885:42-47.

Waters, Frank. *Book of the Hopi.* Penguin Books, New York, 1977.

Wyckoff, Lydia L. (ed). *Visions And Voices: Native American Painting.* Philbroook Museum of Art, Tulsa, 1996.

7: Loss, Restitution and Creativity:The Life of Edvard Munch

Eggum, A. "The Death Theme." *Edvard Munch Symbols and Images.* Eastern Press, New Haven, Conn., 1978:143-183.

Freud, Sigmund. *Mourning and Melancholia.* Standard Edition, Vol. 14:239-258.

Hagman, George, CSW. "Bereavement and Neurosis." *The Journal of the American Academy of Psychoanalysis.* Vol. 23, No. 4, Winter 1995:635-653.

Heller, R. *"Munch: His Life and Work.* University of Chicago Press, Chicago, III., 1984.

Rieder, E.G. "Unresolved Grief Reaction: Edvard Munch." *Psychiatric Annals* 12:3, March 1982.

Messer, T.M. *Edvard Munch.* Harry W. Abrams, New York 1985.

Selz, J.E. *Munch.* Crown Press, New York, 1976.

Stang, R. *Edvard Munch: The Man and His Art.* Abbyville Press, New York, 1977.

Viederman, Milton. "Edvard Munch: A Life in Art." *Journal of the American Academy of Psychoanalysis.* Vol. 22(1) Spring 1994:73-110.

Wolfenstein, Martha. "How Is Mourning Possible?" *The Psychoanalytic Study of the Child,* Vol. 21, International Universities Press, New York, 1966:393-423.

——. "Loss, Rage and Repetition. *Psychoanalytic Study of the Child.* Vol. 24, International Universities Press, New York, 1969:432-460.

8: Living With A Ghost—Vincent Van Gogh's Legacy

Blum, Harold P. "Van Gogh's Chairs." *The American Imago.* Vol. 13, editor George Wilbur Kravs, New York, 1956.

Brooks, C.M. *Vincent Van Gogh: A Biography.* 1942.

Fleming, William. *Art and Ideas.* 6th edition. Holt, Reinhart & Winston, New York, 1980.

Freud, Sigmund. *Doestoevsky & Parricide.* International Journal for Psychoanalysis, Vol. XXVI, 1945.

Gedo, John E. MD. *Portraits of the Artist: Psychoanalysis of Creativity and Its Vicissitudes.* The Guilford Press, New York & London, 1883.

Goldwater, Robert. *Vincent Van Gogh.* Harry N. Abrahms, Inc., 1953.

Graetz, H.R. *The Symbolic Language of Vincent van Gogh,* McGraw-Hill, New York, 1963.

Hibbard, Howard. *The Metropolitan Museum of Art.* New York, 1986. Copyright John Calmann and King Ltd., London.

Holstinjn, Westerman A.J. "The Psychological Development of Vincent Van Gogh." Translated by Hans P. Winzin from *Imago,* Vol. 10, 1924.

Hulsker, J. *The Complete Van Gogh.* H.N. Abrams, New York, 1980.

Meissner, W.W. "Vincent: The Self-Portraits." *The Psychoanalytic Quarterly,* Vol. LXII, 1993, No. 1:74-105.

Nagera, Humberto. *Vincent Van Gogh.* International Universities Press, Inc.,

Madison, Conn., 1990.

Perry, Isabella H. "Vincent Van Gogh: A Case Record." *Bulletin History of Medicine*, 1947, Vol. 21:146-172.

Pierre, D'Espezel and Fosca, Francois. *A Concise Illustrated History of European Painting*. Washington Square Press, Inc., 1961.

Schnier, Jacque. "The Blazing Sun: A Psychoanalytic Approach to Van Gogh." *The American Imago*, Vol. 7, No. 1, March 1950:143-162.

Spitz, Ellen Handler. *Art and Psyche: A Study in Psychoanalysis and Aesthetics*. Yale University Press. New Haven, Conn. & London, 1985.

——. *Art and Psychoanalysis*. Yale University Press, 1985.

Turco, Ronald. "Two Chairs & A Vase: Symbolism in the Art of Van Gogh." *The Psychoanalytic Psychotherapy Review*. Vol. 5, No. 4, 1994:184-189.

Van Gogh-Bonger, J. *The Letters of Vincent Van Gogh to His Brother*. Vol. 1 and 2, London & Boston, 1927.

Waelder, Robert. "The Principle of Multiple Function: Observations on Over-Determination." *Psychoanalytic Quarterly,* 1936, 5:45-62.

9: The Man Who Startled His Contemporaries—Leonardo da Vinci

Anderson, Wayne, Ph.D. "Leonardo da Vinci and the Slip that Fooled Almost Everybody." *Psychoanalysis & Contemporary Thought.* New York, 1994.

Beck, J. *Presentations to Discussion Groups on Psychoanalysis and Art History.* American Psychoanalytic Association, New York, December 12, 1982.

Bramly, Serge. *Leonardo: Discovering the Life of Leonard da Vinci.* Edward Burlingame Books, Harper Collins, New York, 1991.

Clark, K. *Leonardo da Vinci: An Account of his Development as an Artist.* Cambridge Press, 1939.

Coles, Robert. "On Psychohistory." *Psychohistory: Readings in the Method of Psychology, Psychoanalysis and History.* Ed. Geoffrey Colks, Travis L. Crosby. Yale University Press, New Haven, Conn. & London, 1987.

De Voto, G. and Oli, G.C., "Dizionario Della Lingua Italiana." *Le Monnier, Fierenze,* 1971:1496-1497.

Eissler, K.R. *Leonard da Vinci: Psychoanalytic Notes on the Enigma.* International Universities Press, New York, 1961.

Freud, Sigmund. "Leonardo da Vinci and a Memory Of His Childhood." *Standard Edition of the Complete Psychological Works of Sigmund Freud,* Vol. XI (1910). Translated from German under general editor James Strachey in collaboration with Anna Freud. The Hogarth Press and the Institute of Psychoanalysis, London, 1957:57-137.

——. *Inhibitions, Symptoms and Anxiety.* IBID, 1926, S.E.19:226-232.

——. *The Interpretation of Dreams.* S.E. 1900.

Gedo, John. *Portraits of the Artist.* The Guilford Press, New York & London, 1983:15.

Greenacre, Phyllis. *The Childhood of the Artist in Emotional Growth, Vol. 2,* International Universities Press, New York, 1971:479-504.

Holt, Jim. "Leonardo: Discovering the Life of Leonardo da Vinci." *The Wall Street Journal,* Leisure & Arts section, January 3, 1992.

Jones, Ernest. *The Life and Work of Sigmund Freud, Vol. 1.* Anchor Books, Doubleday & Company, Inc., Garden City, New York, 1953.

Kris, Ernst. *Psychoanalytic Explorations in Art.* Yale University School of Medicine. International Universities Press, New York, 1952.

Liebert, R.S. "Michelangelo Dying Slave: A Psychoanalytic Study in Iconography. *The Psychoanalytic Study of the Child.* 1977, 34:463:525.

MacCurdy, E., (ed.) *The Notebooks of Leonardo da Vinci.* Cambridge Press, London, 1938.

Richter, J.P., ed. *The Literary Works of Leonard da Vinci,* Oxford Press, 1977, (3rd edition; 2 vols.), London & New York, 1970.

Shlain, Leonard. *Art and Physics: Parallel Visions in Space, Time and Light.* William Morrow and Co., Inc. New York, 1991.

Spector, Jack J. *The Aesthetics of Freud: A Study in Psychoanalysis and Art.* McGraw-Hill Book Co., New York, 1972.

Shapiro, M. "Leonard and Freud: An Art Historical Study." *Journal of the History of Ideas.* 1956:17:303-36.

Spitz, Ellen Handler. *Art and Psyche: A Study in Psychoanalysis and Aesthetics.* Yale University Press. New Haven, Conn. & London, 1985.

Webster's New Collegiate Dictionary, A Marriam Webster Company, Springfield, Mass. 1956:175, 464 and 672.

10: The End Is The Beginning

Bowlby, J. *Loss: Sadness and Depression. Attachments and Loss.* Basic Books, Inc., New York, 3:137-171.

Brody, S. and Siegel, M. *The Evolution of Character: Birth to 18 Years. A Longitudinal Study.* International Universities Press, Madison, Conn., 1992.

Ford, C.V. *The Somatizing Disorders: Illness as a Way of Life.* Elsevier Biomedical, 1983.

Freud, Sigmund. *The Ego and Id,* Standard Edition, Vol. 19, edited by J. Strachey, London, Hogarth Press, 1922, 1961:3-66.

——. *Civilization and Its Discontents.* Standard Edition, Vol. 21, London, Hogarth Press, 1930.

——. "Problems of Infantile Neurosis." *Psychoanalytic Study of the Child.* International Universities Press.

——. *The Economic Problem of Masochism.* Standard Edition of the Complete Psychological Works of Sigmund Freud, edited by J. Strachey, Hogarth Press and the Institute of Psychoanalysis. Vol, XIX:159-170, 1961.

Greenacre, Phyllis. *Emotional Growth.* Two volumes. International Universities Press, New York, 1971.

Hartman, H. *Ego Psychology and the Problem of Adaptation.* International Universities Press, New York, 1958.

Jacobson, E. *The Self and the Object World.* International Universities Press, 1964.

Kernberg, O.F. "Structure Derivatives of Object Relationships." *International Journal of Psychoanalysis*, 1966, 47:236-253.

——. *Borderline Conditions and Pathological Narcissism.* Jason Aronson, Inc., New York, 1975.

Kohut, H. *The Analysis of the Self: A Systematic Approach to the Psychoanalytic Treatment of Narcissistic Personality Disorders.* International Universities Press, New York, 1971.

Mahler, M.S. and McDevitt, J.B. "Thoughts on the Emergence of the Sense of Self." *Journal of the American Psychoanalytic Association,* 1982, 30:827.

Index

F

family romance 18
fantasy
    18, 34, 51, 67, 72, 99, 108, 118, 126, 133, 141, 142, 146, 157, 166,
    173, 174, 177, 180
Fauvism 135
Fechter, Paul 132
fictive approach 171, 178
Fischer, John 74, 85, 88, 90, 91
Fleming, William 22
Fliess, Wilhelm 47, 171, 182
free associates 153
free-association 172
Freud, Anna 144
Freud, Martha 180, 181
Freud, Sigmund
    17, 18, 43, 47, 127, 171, 173, 174, 175, 176, 178, 179, 181, 182,
    183, 185, 188

G

Gates, Bill 161
Gauguin, Paul
    132, 134, 145, 146, 148, 150, 151, 152, 153, 154, 155, 156, 157
Gedo, John E. 48
Giacomo (also see Salai) 169
Goethe, Johann Wolfgang 180, 181
Goldman, Emma 78
Goldwater, Robert 91, 92
good enough mother 126, 127
good enough mothering 191
Gottlieb, Adolph 83
Greenacre, Phyllis 18, 44, 48, 144, 175, 176, 191
Greer, Sonny 50
Groetz, H.R. 156
Grokest, Albert 72, 93, 95
Guston, Philip 71

H

Hamilton, George Heard 87
Hamlet 155, 171, 174, 181
Hammer, Armand 161
hara-kiri 106, 107
Hardin, Helen 81, **111-124**, 126, 186
Hardin, Herbert 112
Hardin, Margarete 116, 120
Harlem Renaissance 52
Hartmann 171

Hasse, John 35, 52, 53
Helga Collection 30
Hemingway, Ernest 185
Herrera, Joe H. 118
heterophony 38
Hiraoka, Azusa 107
Hiraoka, Kimitake 97
Hiraoka, Mitsuko 101
Homer, Winslow 24
homosexuality 40, 66, 101, 173, 175, 182
Hoving, Thomas 24, 31
Hughes, Robert 22, 23, 88, 89
Hurd, Peter 25
hypochondriasis 68

I

Igo, M. 107
imagination 15, 18
Impressionism 132
Impressionists 146
internal object 143, 182
internalized father 108
internalized relationship 72
intrapsychic 127, 128, 130, 144

J

Jacobson, Daniel 140
Jamieson, Kathleen 30
Jazz 34, 35, 37, 38, 40, 46, 49, 50, 54, 56, 64, 68
Jones, Ernest 180
Joplin, Scott 37, 46, 86
Jung, Carl 113, 121, 133, 171

K

kachinas 112, 113, 114, 115
Kandinsky, Wassily 132
Kawabata, Yasunari 100, 103, 107
Keats, John 125
Kennedy, Flossie 59
Klein, Melanie 192
Kline, Nathan 94
Kris, Ernst 44, 49, 144, 175
Kuerner farm 22, 28, 30
Kunitz, Stanley 81

O

P

R

Ronald Turco, M.D. is a Diplomate of the American Board of Psychiatry and Neurology and Associate Clinical Professor at the Oregon Health Sciences University. As a member of the American Academy of Psychoanalysis, he serves as Chairman of The Study Group on Art, Creativity and Culture, and Vice-Chairman of the Committee on Human Rights and Social Issues. He is active in Transcultural study programs and the sponsorship of children through The Future For Children Program. He serves as President of the American Society of Psychoanalytic Physicians.

Dr. Turco is the author of more than one hundred publications including the book *Closely Watched Shadows: Profile of the Hunter and the Hunted.* He is co-recipient of the Milton Erickson Award For Scientific Writing (1991) and is listed in International Who's Who In Medicine. An amateur artist and photographer, he lives in Portland, Oregon with his wife, Joanne, and his Chow Chow, Louie.

To order additional copies of

ARCHITECTURE OF CREATIVITY: PROFILES BEHIND THE MASK

Send check or money order:
Book: $16.95 plus $3.00 shipping/handling

Imago Books
Dancing Moon Press
P. O. Box 25097
Portland, Oregon 97298
503-803-4373